S0-AWI-004

Quick Reference Guide™

WordPerfect® 6.1

for Windows™

14 East 38 St New York, NY 10016

First Dictation Disc Printing

10 9   8   7

Catalog No. W19

ISBN: 1-56243-257-5

Printed in the United States of America

INTRODUCTION

*Welcome to the **DDC Quick Reference Guide for WordPerfect 6.1 for Windows**. This guide will save you hours searching through technical manuals.*

WordPerfect 6.1 for Windows is an exciting and versatile product. WordPerfect improved familiar features, added new ones, and made it easy to customize both. For example, if you don't like the way the Toolbar appears, you can rearrange the buttons; and, if you want to redesign it entirely, you can do that too. In fact, you can even make the Toolbar disappear if you wish.

Writing about such a versatile product, one you can alter so dramatically to meet your individual needs, is difficult. Since we cannot be sure which, if any, buttons appear on your Toolbar, we always provide keystrokes that will work—no matter how you design your screen.

It is our hope this guide will make it easier for you to use WordPerfect 6.1 for Windows.

Authors: Kathy Berkemeyer   Rebecca Fiala
                Gayle Jensen   Deborah J. Miller
                Marivel Salazar   Karl Schwartz
                Pamela R. Toliver

Managing Editor: Kathy Berkemeyer

Assistant Editor: Rebecca Fiala

Layout: DDC Publishing

TABLE OF CONTENTS

continued

TABLE OF CONTENTS (continued)

continued...

iv

TABLE OF CONTENTS (continued)

continued

V

TABLE OF CONTENTS (continued)

continued...

vi

vii

TABLE OF CONTENTS (continued)

continued...

viii

TABLE OF CONTENTS (continued)

continued.

TABLE OF CONTENTS (continued)

continued...

X

TABLE OF CONTENTS (continued)

continued.

TABLE OF CONTENTS (continued)

continued...

xii

continued

xiii

TABLE OF CONTENTS (continued)

continued.

xiv

continued

XV

TABLE OF CONTENTS (continued)

continued

TABLE OF CONTENTS (continued)

continued

xvii

continued...

xviii

TABLE OF CONTENTS (continued)

ABBREVIATIONS

Helps you type standard information quickly (e.g., letter closing, company address, etc.).

First, assign standard information to abbreviation. Then, whenever you want this information, type abbreviation and expand (see page 2).

(See TEMPLATES, page 250.)

Create Abbreviation

1. Enter and select information to assign to abbreviation.

2. Select <u>I</u>nsert menu .... `Alt`+`I`

3. Select **Abbreviations** .... `A`

4. Click `Create...` .... `Enter`

5. Type **Abbreviation Name** .... *text*
   in text box.

   NOTE: Abbreviations are case sensitive.

6. Click `OK` .... `Enter`

7. Click `Close` .... `Alt`+`C`

Insert Abbreviation

1. Place insertion point where data is to appear.

2. Type abbreviation .... *text*

   *NOTE: Abbreviations can be expanded
   immediately or at some future time.*

Expand Abbreviation

1. Place insertion point in abbreviation, or select it.

2. Press **Ctrl+A** .... `Ctrl`+`A`

Change Abbreviation Text

1. Select new text.

2. Select **Insert** menu .... `Alt`+`I`

3. Select **Abbreviations** .... `A`

4. Select abbreviation .... `Alt`+`A`, `↑` `↓`
    to replace.

5. Click [**Replace**] .... `Alt`+`L`

6. Click [**Yes**] .... `Y`

7. Click [**Close**] .... `Alt`+`C`

Copy Abbreviation Between Templates

1. Select **Insert** menu .... `Alt`+`I`

2. Select **Abbreviations** .... `A`

3. Click [**Copy...**] . ... `Alt`+`O`

4. Select **Template to Copy from** .... `F4`, `↑` `↓`

5. Select abbreviation .... `Alt`+`S`, `↑` `↓`
    to copy.

continued.

Copy Abbreviation Between Templates (continued)

6. Select **Template** .... Alt+T, F4, ↑ ↓
   to Copy to.

7. Click [**Copy**] .... Alt+C

8. Click [**Close**] .... Alt+C

ADVANCE

Advances text to an exact location on the page.

Advance Text

1. Place insertion point where Advance is to begin.

2. Select **Format** menu .... Alt+R

3. Select **Typesetting** .... T

4. Select **Advance** .... A

5. Select desired **Horizontal Position**.

6. Enter inches to advance .... Alt+Z, *number*
   in **Horizontal Distance** text box.

   NOTE: Units used in this dialog box are set by
   ***Display Preferences**. (See*
   ***PREFERENCES**, page 170, for more*
   information.)

7. Choose desired **Vertical Position**.

   **To place text below position, select from top of
   page (rather than above it):**

   Deselect **Text Above Position** .... Alt+P

continued...

4

Advance Text (continued)

8. Enter inches to advance........... **Alt**+**V**, *number* in **Vertical Distance** text box.

9. Click [**OK**] .... **Enter**

APPEND

Adds selected information to data already on Windows clipboard.

1. Select information to append.

2. Select **Edit** menu..................................... **Alt**+**E**

3. Select **Append**... **D**

> *NOTE:* *Information stays on clipboard until you paste it into another WordPerfect document or another Windows application.*

BACKUP

*(See **PREFERENCES**, page 170.)*

BAR CODE

*Creates **POSTNET** (Postal Numeric Encoding Technique) bar codes, meeting U.S. Postal Service specifications.*

Create Bar Code (Envelope)

1. Select **Format** menu .... **Alt**+**R**

continued.

Create Bar Code (Envelope) (continued)

2. Select En**v**elope ....

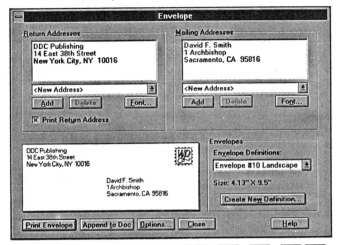

3. Select desired size.......... **Alt** + **V**, **F4**, **↑** **↓**
   from En**v**elope
   Definitions drop–down list.

4. Type return address ...... **Alt** + **R**, *return address*

5. Type mailing.................... **Alt** + **M**, *mailing address*
   address.

   *NOTE: Include either the ZIP Code, the ZIP+4
   Code, or the 11–digit Delivery Point Bar
   Code (DPBC).*

6. Click **Options...** .... **Alt** + **O**

7. Select desired **USPS POSTNET Bar Code Option**.

8. Click **OK** .... **Enter**

continued...

6

Create Bar Code (Envelope) (continued)

*NOTE: Notice the code you typed in step 5 is
inserted in **POSTNET Bar Code** text box.*

To print envelope and return to document:

Click `Print Envelope` .... `Enter`

To insert address information (with bar code) at end of document:

Click `Append to Doc` .... `Alt`+`T`

To cancel Envelope dialog box and return to document:

Click `Close` .... `Alt`+`C`

Add Bar Code to Text

1. Place insertion point where bar code is to appear.

2. Select **Insert** menu .... `Alt`+`I`

3. Select **Other**.. `O`

4. Select **Bar Code** .... `B`

5. Enter desired postal code when **Bar Code Digits** text box appears.

```
┌────────────────────────────────────────────┐
│ ▭            POSTNET Bar Code               │
├────────────────────────────────────────────┤
│                                             │
│  Enter an 11-digit Delivery Point Bar   ┌──────┐ │
│  Code, a 5-digit ZIP Code, or a         │  OK  │ │
│  9-digit (ZIP + 4).                     └──────┘ │
│                                         ┌──────┐ │
│  Bar Code Digits:                       │Cancel│ │
│  ┌─────────────────────────┐            └──────┘ │
│  │ 60513                   │            ┌──────┐ │
│  └─────────────────────────┘            │ Help │ │
│                                         └──────┘ │
└────────────────────────────────────────────┘
```

6. Click `OK` .... `Enter`

Change Bar Code in Document

1. Place insertion point at end of bar code and click.

2. Press **Backspace**..................................`Backspace`

3. Complete steps 2–6 of **Add Bar Code to Text**, page 6.

BASELINE PLACEMENT

> *CAUTION: Baseline placement affects the entire document.*

1. Select **Fo_r_mat** menu............................`Alt`+`R`

2. Select **_T_ypesetting** ....`T`

3. Select **_W_ord/Letter Spacing**.........................`W`

4. Select **_B_aseline Placement**..................`Alt`+`B`
   for Typesetting check box.

5. Click `OK` ....`Enter`

BEEP ON/OFF

(See PREFERENCES, page 170.)

BINDING OPTIONS

(See PRINT, page 171, for more information.)

1. Select **Fo_r_mat** menu............................`Alt`+`R`

2. Select **_P_age** ....`P`

3. Select **B_i_nding/Duplex** ....`I`

4. Select edge from which to shift.

continued...

8

BINDING OPTIONS (continued)

5. Enter space to shift.............. `Alt`+`A`, *number*
   in **Amount** text box.

6. Select desired .... `Alt`+`D`, `F4`, `↑` `↓`
   Duplexing option if your
   printer supports this feature.

7. Click `OK` .... `Enter`

BLOCK PROTECT

1. Select text to protect from soft page break.

2. Select **Format** menu .... `Alt`+`R`

3. Select **Page**.. `P`

4. Select **Keep Text Together** .... `K`

5. Select/deselect **Keep selected text**........ `Alt`+`K`
   together on same page check box.

6. Click `OK` .... `Enter`

BOLD

Bold Existing Text

1. Select desired text .... `Shift`, `↑` `↓` `←` `→`

2. Click `b` ....`Ctrl`+`B`
   on default Toolbar.

   OR

   a. Click **Format**............................... `Alt`+`R`

   b. Click **Bold**.................................. `Alt`+`B`

Bold New Text

1. Click ⬚**b** .... `Ctrl`+`B`
   on default Toolbar.

2. Type text.. *text*

3. Click ⬚**b** .... `Ctrl`+`B`
   to turn bold off.

BOOKMARKS

*Holds your place in a document. You must assign a name to each bookmark. A generic bookmark, called a **QuickMark**, can also be used in a document.*

> *NOTE: Bookmarks are also used in Hypertext links. (See **HYPERTEXT**, page 100.)*

Set QuickMark

1. Place cursor where you wish to insert QuickMark.

2. Select **Insert** menu .... `Alt`+`I`

3. Select **Bookmark** .... `B`

4. Click ⬚ **Set QuickMark** .... `Alt`+`Q`

   > *NOTE: You can have only one QuickMark in a document.*

Find QuickMark

1. Select **Insert** menu .... `Alt`+`I`

2. Select **Bookmark** .... `B`

3. Click ⬚ **Find QuickMark** .... `Alt`+`F`

Create Bookmark

1. Place cursor where bookmark is to appear.

2. Select **Insert** menu .... `Alt`+`I`

3. Select **Bookmark** .... `B`

4. Click `Create...` .... `Enter`

5. Type **Bookmark Name** .... *text*
   in text box, if desired.

6. Click `OK` .... `Enter`

   To mark selected text as bookmark:

   a. Select text.

   b. Complete steps 2–6, above.

Find Bookmark

1. Select **Insert** menu .... `Alt`+`I`

2. Select **Bookmark** .... `B`

3. Select bookmark .... `↓` `↑`
   to find.

   To move to bookmark:

   Click `Go To` .... `Alt`+`G`

   To move to bookmark and select text:

   Click `Go To & Select` .... `Alt`+`S`

Rename Bookmark

1 Select **Insert** menu .... `Alt`+`I`

2. Select **Bookmark** .... `B`

3. Select bookmark.................................. `↑` `↓`
   to rename.

4. Click ⎿ **Rename...** ⏌ .... `Alt`+`R`

5. Type new **Bookmark Name** .... *text*
   in text box.

6. Click ⎿ **OK** ⏌ .... `Enter`

7. Click ⎿ **Close** ⏌ .... `Alt`+`C`

Move Bookmark

1. Place cursor where you would like to move
   bookmark.

2. Select **Insert** menu .... `Alt`+`I`

3. Select **Bookmark** .... `B`

4. Select bookmark.................................. `↑` `↓`
   to move.

5. Click ⎿ **Move** ⏌ .... `Alt`+`M`

Delete Bookmark

1. Select **Insert** menu .... `Alt`+`I`

2. Select **Bookmark** .... `B`

3. Select bookmark................................`↑``↓`
   to delete.

4. Click `Delete...` .... `Alt`+`D`

5. Click `Yes` .... `Y`

6. Click `Close` .... `Alt`+`C`

BORDERS

Add Column Border

1. Place insertion point anywhere in column.

   NOTE: Border surrounds all columns in document.

2. Select **Format** menu .... `Alt`+`R`

3. Select **Columns** .... `C`

4. Select **Border/Fill** .... `B`

5. Select style from **Border Style** palette or drop–down list.

6. Select style from **Fill Style** palette or drop–down list.

continued

If you selected a gradient or pattern fill style in step 6:

a. Select color from **Foreground** palette.

b. Select color from **Background** palette.

7. Click [**OK**] .... [Enter]

Add Paragraph Border

1. Place insertion point in paragraph to frame.

2. Select **Format** menu .... [Alt]+[R]

3. Select **Paragraph** .... [A]

4. Select **Border/Fill** .... [B]

5. Select style from **Border Style** palette or drop–down list.

6. Select style from **Fill Style** palette or drop–down list.

   If you selected a gradient or pattern fill style in step 6:

   a. Select color from **Foreground** palette.

   b. Select color from **Background** palette.

7. Click [**OK**] .... [Enter]

Add Page Border

1. Place insertion point on first page to frame.

   NOTE: Border appears on all subsequent pages in document.

2. Select **Fo_r_mat** menu .... `Alt`+`R`

3. Select **_P_age** .... `P`

4. Select **_B_order/Fill** .... `B`

5. Select style from **_B_order Style** palette or drop–down list.

6 Select style from **_F_ill Style** palette or drop–down list.

   If you selected a gradient or pattern fill style in step 6:

   a. Select color from **Fo_r_eground** palette.

   b. Select color from **B_a_ckground** palette.

7. Click `  OK  ` .... `Enter`

Customize Border

1. Complete steps 1–4 of **Add Column Border, Add Paragraph Border** or **Add Page Border**, above.

2. Click [**Customize Style...**] .... Alt + C

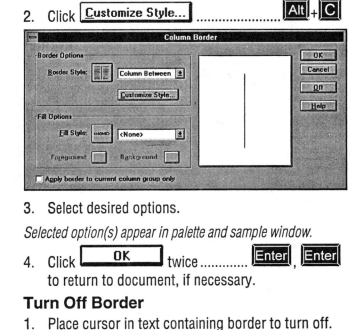

3. Select desired options.

Selected option(s) appear in palette and sample window.

4. Click [**OK**] twice .... Enter, Enter
to return to document, if necessary.

Turn Off Border

1. Place cursor in text containing border to turn off.

2. Select **Format** menu .... Alt + R

3. Select **Paragraph**, **Page** or **Columns**, as needed.

4. Select **Border/Fill** .... B

5. Click [**Off**]

16

BULLETS & NUMBERS

NOTE: Numbers increment automatically.

Apply Bullets & Numbers—New Text

1. Select **Insert** menu .... 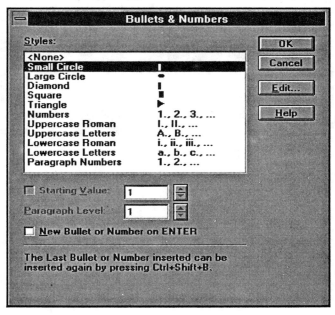Alt + I

2. Select **Bullets & Numbers** .... N

3. Select desired bullet or number style......... ↑ ↓

    If you selected a number style in step 3:

    a. Select **Starting Value** check box ..... Alt + V

    b. Enter beginning number...................... *number*

continued

Apply Bullets & Numbers—New Text (continued)

To insert new bullet or number on Enter:

Select **New Bullet or Number** .... `Alt`+`N`
on ENTER check box.

4. Click `OK` .... `Enter`

Apply Bullets & Numbers—Existing Text

1. Select text to which you would like to apply bullets or numbers.

2. Select **Insert** menu .... `Alt`+`I`

3. Select **Bullets & Numbers** .... `N`

4. Select desired bullet or number style.

5. Click `OK` .... `Enter`

Edit Bullets & Numbers

NOTE: *You can edit predefined bullet and number styles with the Styles Editor. (See **STYLES**, page 206.)*

CENTER

*(See **JUSTIFICATION**, page 114, also.)*

Center Text

1. Place insertion point where centering is to begin.

2. Click `≢` .... `Shift`+`F7`
   on Format Toolbar.

   NOTE: *To center text with a dot leader, press **Shift+F7** twice.*

continued...

Center Text (continued)

3. Type text (maximum one line) .... *text*

   NOTE: You can center more than once on a line, as long as text is separated by a tab or more than one space.

End Centering/Alignment

Ends centering in the middle of a line to allow text to be typed on the same line.

1. Select **Fo_r_mat** menu .... `Alt`+`R`

2. Select **_L_ine**.......................... `L`

3. Select **_O_ther Codes**.......................... `O`

4. Select **End Centering/Alignment**.......................... `G`

5. Click `Insert` .... `Enter`

Center Text on Next Tab Stop

1. Select **Fo_r_mat** menu .... `Alt`+`R`

2. Select **_L_ine**.......................... `L`

3. Select **_O_ther Codes**.......................... `O`

   To center over tab stop:

   Select **_C_enter** .... `C`

   To center over tab stop and add dot leader:

   Select **Ce_n_ter** .... `N`

4. Click `Insert` .... `Enter`

Center Page (Top to Bottom)

1. Place insertion point at top of page to center.

2. Select 🖽 .... `Alt`+`R`, `P`, `C`
   on Page Toolbar.

3. Select **Current <u>P</u>age** .... `P`

   OR

   Select **Current and <u>S</u>ubsequent Pages** .... `S`

4. Click [**OK**] .... `Enter`

CLOSE

Close Document

Press **Ctrl+F4** .... `Ctrl`+`F4`

If Save Changes to Document message appears:

Click [**No**] .... `N`

to close document without saving changes.

OR

Select [**Yes**] .... `Y`

to save document.

If Save As dialog box appears:

NOTE: A **Save As** *dialog box appears only if you are working on a new document.*

a. Type filename .... *filename*

NOTE: Type a path, if necessary.

b. Click [**OK**] .... `Enter`

OR

Click [**Cancel**] .... `Esc`

20

Close (Exit) WordPerfect

1. Press **Alt+F4** .... `Alt`+`F4`

   If Save Changes to Document message appears:

   Click `No` .... `N`

   to exit without saving changes.

   OR

   a. Click `Yes` .... `Y`

      to save changes and exit.

   b. Type filename .... *filename*

      in **Save As** text box.

   NOTE: Type a path, if necessary.

   c. Click `OK` .... `Enter`

2. Repeat above steps for each document to close.

COACH

Gives you interactive assistance for a procedure while you complete it. When you use this special feature of WordPerfect Help, you are actually performing the tasks, not practicing.

1. Click  .... Alt + H , O
2. Select desired topic from the list.

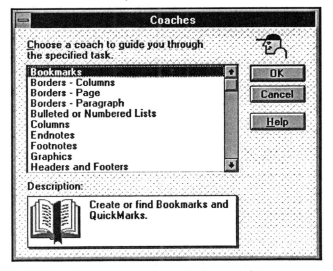

3. Follow the onscreen prompts to complete your procedure.

COLUMNS

NOTE: You can have up to 24 columns on a page.

Column Types

There are four basic column types:

- Newspaper

  Flows down to bottom of the first column and up to the top of next one.

- Balanced Newspaper

  Flows down to bottom of the first column and up to top of the next one. Each column is of equal length, however.

- Parallel

  Groups text across the page in rows. The next row starts below the longest column of the previous row.

- Parallel with Block Protect

  Keeps each row of columns together. If a column in one row becomes so long it moves to the next page, the entire row moves with it.

Define/Turn On Columns

NOTE: If a definition has been specified in a document, you can use this procedure to change it or turn it on.

1. Place insertion point where columns are to begin.

2. Select **Format** menu .... **Alt**+**R**

   OR

   —FROM POWER BAR—

   a. Click `Columns ▼`

   b. Click desired number of columns.

   OR

   Click **Define** and skip to steps 5–8 below.

Define/Turn On Columns (continued)

continu

3. Select **Columns** C

4. Select **Define** .... D

Columns

Number of Columns
Columns: 2

OK
Cancel
Help

Type
- Newspaper
- Balanced Newspaper
- Parallel
- Parallel w/Block Protect

Column Spacing

Spacing Between Columns:
0.500"

Line Spacing Between
Rows In Parallel Columns:
1

Column Widths

	Width	Fixed
Column 1:	3"	☐
Space:	0.500"	☒
Column 2:	3"	☐

5. Enter desired number of **Columns** .... *number*

6. Choose desired column **Type** option.

    To set default spacing between columns:

    a. Select **Spacing Between Columns** .... Alt + S

    b. Enter desired measurement .... *number*

    *NOTE: If you selected **Parallel** in step 6, select*
    Line Spacing Between Rows In Parallel
    ***Columns** and enter desired measurement.*

    This option is only available for two
    different parallel column settings.

7. Change **Column Widths** settings, if desired.

8. Click [OK] .... Enter

Insert Column Break

Press **Ctrl+Enter**...................................... `Ctrl` + `Enter`
to insert column break.

Move from Column to Column

TO MOVE: PRESS:

To top of column.................................. `Alt` + `Home`

To last line of column .... `Alt` + `End`

To previous column.............................. `Alt` + `←`

To next column...................................... `Alt` + `→`

Turn Columns Off

1. Place cursor where you want to turn off columns.

2. Select **Format** menu .... `Alt` + `R`
   OR

   —FROM POWER BAR—

   a. Click `Columns ▼`

   b. Click **Columns Off**.

3. Select **Columns** .... `C`

4. Click **Off** .... `O`

Delete Column Definition

1. Turn on **Reveal Codes** *(see REVEAL CODES, page 184)*.

2. Place cursor directly after column definition code.

3. Press **Backspace** .... `Backspace`

COMMENTS

Adds non–printing information to a document. For every comment you create, a comment icon appears in the margin. This icon can be customized (see PREFERENCES, page 170).

In Draft view, comments are displayed in highlight bars. In Page view, click the comment icon to see the comment.

Create Comment

> *NOTE: You can use most WordPerfect formatting and text attribute features in a comment.*

1. Select text to convert to comment.
   OR
   Place cursor where you wish to place comment.

2. Select **I**nsert menu .... **Alt** + **I**

3. Select **Co**m**ment** .... **M**

4. Select **C**reate .... **C**

5. Type comment text .... *text*

6. Choose desired options to include additional information.

   > *NOTE: **I**nitials and **Na**me options are only available if specified under **E**nvironment **Preferences**.*

   To move to the next comment:
   Click [Next] .... **Shift** + **Alt** + **N**

   To move to the previous comment:
   Click [Previous] .... **Shift** + **Alt** + **P**

continued...

Create Comment (continued)

7. Click [**Close**] .... Shift + Alt + C
   to return to document.

Edit Comment

1. Place insertion point after comment code to edit.

   *NOTE: Turn on Reveal Codes, if necessary. (See **REVEAL CODES**, page 184.)*

2. Select **Insert** menu .... Alt + I

3. Select **Comment** .... M

   NOTE: In Page view mode, you can also double-click the comment icon. You must, however, be able to view the margins.

4. Select **Edit** .... E

5. Edit the comment.

6. Click [**Close**] .... Shift + Alt + C
   to return to document.

Convert Comment to Text

1. Place cursor after comment code to convert.

   *NOTE: Turn on Reveal Codes, if necessary. (See **REVEAL CODES**, page 184.)*

2. Select **Insert** menu .... Alt + I

3. Select **Comment** .... M

4. Select **Convert to Text** .... T

COMPARE DOCUMENT

Compares current document with previous version, marks deleted, moved or new text. Changes are not marked in comments, footers, graphics boxes, headers or watermarks, however.

To indicate changed text, WordPerfect uses the following methods:

- *Deleted information* is struck out.

- *Moved information* is introduced and followed by a message indicating it was moved.

- *Added information* is redlined.

1. Open new version of document to compare.

2. Select **File** menu .... Alt + F

3. Select **Compare Document** .... R

4. Select **Add Markings** .... A

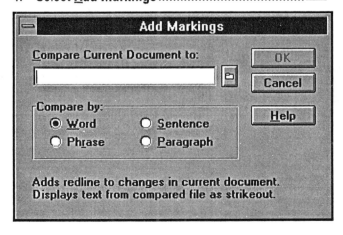

continued...

COMPARE DOCUMENT (continued)

5. Choose desired **Compare by** option.

6. Click 🖻 to compare open document with old version on disk or document under different filename.

7. Type document path .... *path, filename* and filename.

8. Click **⬛ OK** twice .... Enter, Enter

Remove Marks

1. Open document from which you would like to remove markings.

2. Select **File** menu .... Alt + F

3. Select **Compare Document** .... R

4. Select **Remove Markings** .... R

   To remove all markings:

   Select **Remove Redline Markings** .... R
   and Strikeout Text.

   To keep markings for new text/remove all others:

   Select **Remove Strikeout Text Only** .... S

5. Click **⬛ OK** .... Enter

Change Appearance of Redline Text

1. Select **Format** menu .... Alt + R

2. Select **Document** .... D

3. Select **Redline Method** .... R

4. Choose desired **Method** option:

   - **Printer Dependent** .... Enter
     to use redline specific to your printer.

   - **Mark Left Margin** L
     to mark left margin.

   - **Mark Alternating Margins** .... A
     to mark left margin for even-numbered
     pages and right margin for odd-numbered
     pages.

   - **Mark Right Margin** .... R
     to mark right margin.

   *NOTE: Type a new character in **Redline Character**
   text box if you choose one of the above
   margin options and want to mark text with
   something other than displayed character.*

   - | Use as Default | .... Alt + A

     to use current redline
     settings as default

5. Click | OK | .... Enter

CONDITIONAL END OF PAGE

1. Place cursor on line above text to keep together.

2. Select **Format** menu .... `Alt`+`R`

3. Select **Page** .... `P`

4. Select **Keep Text Together** .... `K`

5. Select **Number of lines** .... `Alt`+`N`
   to keep together.

6. Enter **Number of lines** .... *number*
   to keep together in text box.

7. Click `      OK      ` .... `Enter`

CONVERT CASE

Converts text to upper– or lowercase letters.

> *NOTE:* *When converting to initial capitals, words
> like "and" and "the" remain in lowercase.
> When converting to lowercase, words
> starting with "I" (e.g., "I'd," "I'm," etc.) and
> the first word of each sentence remains
> uppercase.*

1. Select text to convert.

2. Select **Edit** menu .... `Alt`+`E`

3. Select **Convert Case** .... `V`

4. Choose desired option.

COPY OR CUT (MOVE) DATA

*(See **APPEND**, page 4; **DRAG AND DROP**, page 50, for more information.)*

1. Select text and/or graphics box.

2. Click 🖺 .... **Ctrl**+**C**
   to copy data.

   OR

   Click ✂ .... **Ctrl**+**X**
   to cut data.

   —IN DOCUMENT WINDOW OR APPLICATION TO RECEIVE DATA—

3. Place insertion point where you want to insert data.

4. Click 📋 .... **Ctrl**+**V**

   NOTE: Selected data remains on clipboard until replaced with another selection.

COUNTERS

Numbers or counts any item in a document. You can count with numbers, uppercase letters, lowercase letters and upper- and lowercase Roman numerals. Unlike page numbering and figure numbering, however, counters do not work automatically.

Create Counter

1. Select **I**nsert menu .... **Alt**+**I**

2. Select **O**ther .... **O**

3. Select **C**ounter.................................... **C**

continued…

32

Create Counter (continued)

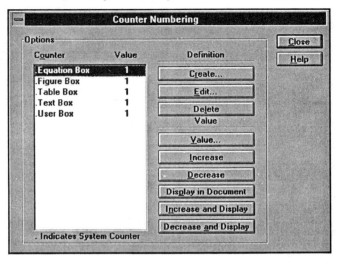

4. Click **Create...** .... **Alt**+**R**

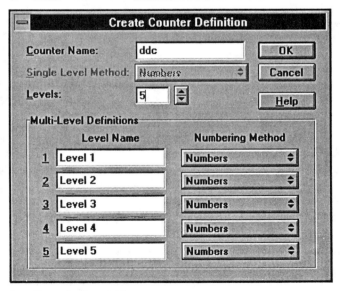

5. Type **Counter Name** .... *name*

continued.

To change single level method of numbering:

Select method .... Alt + S, F4, ↑ ↓
from list.

To change numbering method for multilevel:

a. Select **Levels** .... Alt + L, *number*
   and enter number of levels.

b. Select **Numbering**
   Method .... Alt + *number*, Tab F4, ↓ ↑
   for each level.

6. Click [OK] .... Enter

   AND/OR

   Click [Cancel]

7. Click [Close] .... Alt + C

Display Counters

1. Select **Insert** menu .... Alt + I

2. Select **Other** .... O

3. Select **Counter** C

4. Select desired counter or counter level.

5. Click [Display in Document] .... Alt + P

CROSS–REFERENCE

You must create three different items to produce cross-references:

- **Reference**   *Refers the reader to another section in the document.*
- **Target**   *The location to which you are referring the reader.*
- **Target name**   *The text that ties the reference and the target together.*

   NOTE: The target name is used only to generate cross–references. It is not printed.

To create a cross–reference, you must mark references, targets and target names. You must also generate the cross-references. These procedures are outlined below.

Mark Reference

1. Place insertion point where reference is to appear.

   To display Cross–Reference feature bar:

   a. Select **Tools** menu .... `Alt`+`T`

   b. Select **Cross–Reference** .... `F`

   The Cross–Reference feature bar appears.

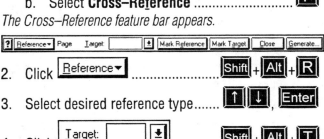

2. Click `Reference▼` .... `Shift`+`Alt`+`R`
3. Select desired reference type....... `↑` `↓`, `Enter`
4. Click `Target:` `±` .... `Shift`+`Alt`+`T`
5. Select target from list .... *target name*

   NOTE: The target name must be the same for the reference and the target.

continued.

Mark Reference (continued)

6. Click ⌷Mark Reference⌷ .... ⌷Shift⌷+⌷Alt⌷+⌷E⌷

Mark Target

1. Place insertion point immediately after target.

   NOTE: *Turn on Reveal Codes, if necessary. (See* ***REVEAL CODES****, page 184, for more information.)*

—*WITH CROSS–REFERENCE FEATURE BAR ACTIVE*—

2. Select target .... *target name* from list.

   NOTE: *The target name must be the same for the target and the reference.*

3. Click ⌷Mark Target⌷ .... ⌷Shift⌷+⌷Alt⌷+⌷A⌷

Generate Cross–References

   NOTE: *A question mark (?) appears in the location of every cross–reference until you generate. (See* ***GENERATE****, page 72, for more information.)*

—*WITH CROSS–REFERENCE FEATURE BAR ACTIVE*—

1. Click ⌷Generate...⌷ .... ⌷Shift⌷+⌷Alt⌷+⌷G⌷

2. Click ⌷ **OK** ⌷ .... ⌷Enter⌷

3. Click ⌷ **Close** ⌷ .... ⌷Shift⌷+⌷Alt⌷+⌷C⌷
   to return to document.

DATE

Insert Date

> *NOTE:* *The date is determined by your computer clock. If the date displayed is incorrect, refer to your DOS manual to set the date and time on your computer.*

1. Place cursor where you would like to place date.

2. Press **Ctrl+D** .... `Ctrl`+`D`
   to insert current date as text.

   OR

   Press **Ctrl+Shift+D** .... `Ctrl`+`Shift`+`D`
   to insert current date as code.

Predefined Date Format

1. Select **Insert** menu .... `Alt`+`I`

2. Select **Date** .... `D`

3. Select **Date Format** .... `F`

4. Select desired format .... `↑` `↓`

5. Click `OK` .... `Enter`

Custom Date/Time Format

1. Select **Insert** menu .... `Alt`+`I`

2. Select **Date** .... `D`

continued.

37

Custom Date/Time Format (continued)

3. Select **Date Format** .... **F**

4. Click **Custom...** .... **Alt**+**C**

5. Place insertion point............... **Alt**+**E**, **←** **→**
   in **Edit Date Format** box
   where new code appears,
   or delete codes, if necessary.

6. Select desired **Date Codes** ...... **Alt**+**D**, **↑** **↓**

7. Click **Insert** .... **Alt**+**I**

8. Add space or punctuation.............. **Alt**+**E**, *text*
   in **Edit Date Format** text box.
   AND/OR

   a. Select **Time/Code** .... **Alt**+**T**, **↑** **↓**

   b. Click **Insert** .... **Alt**+**I**

   c. Add space or punctuation in text box......... *text*

9. Repeat steps 4–6 for each code to add.

10. Click **OK** .... **Enter**

DELAY CODES

Inserts codes to take effect in a specified number of pages.

> *NOTE:* *You can delay open codes or graphs. You cannot delay paired codes or certain typing codes (e.g., Indent, Center, Flush Right, etc.), however.*

Create Delay Code

1. Place cursor in page in which to delay codes.

2. Select **Format** menu .... `Alt`+`R`

3. Select **Page** .... `P`

4. Select **Delay Codes** .... `D`

5. Enter **Number of Pages to Delay** .... *number*

6. Click `OK` .... `Enter`

| `Image...` | `Paper Size...` | `Header/Footer...` | `Watermark...` | `Close` |

7. Choose desired options from Delay Codes feature bar and/or menus.

8. Click `Close` .... `Shift`+`Alt`+`C`
   to return to your document.

DELETE CODES

NOTE: Turn on Reveal Codes, if necessary.

1. Place insertion point in front of code to delete.

2. Press **Delete** .... `Del`

OR

1. Place insertion point after code to delete.

2. Press **Backspace** .... `Backspace`

DELETE TEXT

TO DELETE:	PRESS:
Next character	Del
Previous character	Backspace
Word at insertion point	Ctrl + Backspace
Part of word to right of insertion point	Ctrl + Shift + →, Del
Part of word to left of insertion point	Ctrl + Shift + ←, Del
End of line	Shift + End, Del
End of page	Shift + Alt + Page Down, Del
Selected text	Del

DIRECTORIES—LOCATING FILES

Directories are named locations in which files are stored. A *subdirectory* is a directory stored inside another directory. When a file is not in the current directory, you must specify the path to the file, as shown below.

> *EXAMPLE: c:\wpc\doc*

Specify Location of Files Using Directories List Box

—FROM OPEN OR SAVE AS DIALOG BOX—

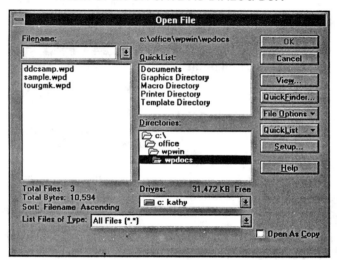

1. Double–click desired directory in **Directories** list box.

   NOTE: To change to a directory above current parent directory, double–click 📁 **c:** *at top of list.*

2. Repeat step 1 until desired directory current.

Files in specified directory appear in Files list box.

Specify Location of Files Using Filename Text Box

—FROM OPEN FILE OR SAVE AS DIALOG BOX—

1. Select **Filename** text box..................... **Alt**+**N**
2. Type path to file(s)..*path*

   EXAMPLE: c:\wpc\doc

continued

Specify Location of Files Using Filename Box (cont)

To limit display to specific file types:

Type filename pattern .... *filespec*
in **Filename** text box.

EXAMPLE: *.LTR

3. Click [OK] .... Enter

Files in specified directory appear in the Filename list box.

View File from Dialog Box
   —FROM OPEN FILE OR SAVE AS DIALOG BOX—

1. Click filename to select .... Alt + N , Tab
    in **Filename** list box.

2. Click [View...] .... Alt + W

A View window opens, displaying contents of selected file.

Delete File(s)
   —FROM OPEN OR SAVE AS DIALOG BOX—

1. Select file(s) .... Tab , ↑ ↓
2. Click [File Options ▼] .... Alt + O , F4
3. Select **Delete** .... Del
4. Click [Delete] .... Alt + D

Copy File

—FROM OPEN FILE OR SAVE AS DIALOG BOX—

1. Select file... `Tab`, `↑` `↓`
2. Click `File Options ▼` .... `Alt`+`O`, `F4`
3. Select **Copy**.. `C`
4. Select directory............................... *path, filename*
   to which you want to copy file.
5. Click `OK` .... `Enter`
6. Select **Don't replace files**...................... `Alt`+`D`
   with the same size, date, and time if you do not
   want to create a file identical to the one being
   copied.
7. Click `Copy` .... `Alt`+`C`

Move File

—FROM OPEN FILE OR SAVE AS DIALOG BOX—

1. Select file... `Tab`, `↑` `↓`
2. Click `File Options ▼` .... `Alt`+`O`, `F4`
3. Select **Move**.. `M`
4. Select directory............................... *path, filename*
   to which you want
   to move file.
5. Click `OK` .... `Enter`
6. Click `Move` .... `Alt`+`M`

Rename File

—FROM OPEN FILE OR SAVE AS DIALOG BOX—

1. Select file.. `Tab`, `↑` `↓`
2. Click `File Options ▼` .... `Alt`+`O`, `F4`
3. Select **R**ename... `R`
4. Select directory ....*path, filename*
   of file to rename.
5. Click `OK` .... `Enter`
6. Click `Rename` .... `Alt`+`R`

Print File(s)

—FROM OPEN FILE OR SAVE AS DIALOG BOX—

1. Select file.. `Tab`, `↑` `↓`
2. Click `File Options ▼` .... `Alt`+`O`, `F4`
3. Select **P**rint... `P`
4. Click `Print` .... `Alt`+`P`

Print File List

—FROM OPEN FILE OR SAVE AS DIALOG BOX—

To print list of only certain files:

Select desired files .... `↑` `↓`, `Enter`
1. Click `File Options ▼` .... `Alt`+`O`, `F4`
   to print entire list.

continued...

44

Print File List (continued)

2. Select **Print File List**.............................. 🔲

3. Choose desired option(s).

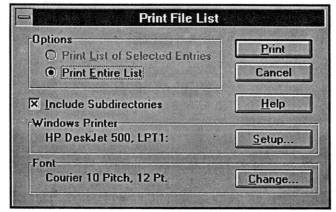

4. Click [**Print**] .... Alt + P

Create Directory

—FROM OPEN FILE OR SAVE AS DIALOG BOX—

1. Select desired drive/directory ...... 🔼🔽, Enter
   in **Drives** drop–down box
   and **Directories** list box.

2. Click [File Options ▼] .... Alt + O , F4

3. Select **Create Directory** .... 🔲

4. Type directory name .... *directory name*
   in **New Directory** text box.

5. Click [**Create**] .... Alt + C

Remove Directory

—FROM OPEN FILE OR SAVE AS DIALOG BOX—

> *CAUTION:* *If you remove a directory containing files or subdirectories, you will not be able to recover the data.*

1. Select directory to delete.............. ⬆ ⬇ , Enter
   in **Directories** list box.

   > *NOTE:* *If you do not specify a directory, the default is the current directory.*

2. Click ⎡ **File Options** ▾ ⎤ .... Alt + O , F4

3. Select **Re**move Directory .... E

4. Click ⎡ **Remove** ⎤ .... Alt + R

DOCUMENT COMPARE

(See COMPARE DOCUMENT, page 27.)

DOCUMENT SUMMARY

A document summary is information (e.g., typist, subject, keywords, etc.) attached to a document. Usually, this information is saved as part of the document and is not printed. It can, however, be saved as a separate file and printed later.

Create Document Summary

1 Select **F**ile menu .... Alt + F

continued...

Create Document Summary (continued)

2. Select **Document Summary**.............................. Y

To fill fields based on document:

a. Click Options ▼ .... Alt + O , F4

b. Select **Extract Information** .... E
   From Document.

To complete remaining fields:

a. Select field.............................. Alt + D , Tab

b. Enter/edit information .... *data*

3. Click OK .... Enter

Delete Document Summary

1. Select **File** menu................................... Alt + F

2. Select **Document Summary**.......................... Y

3. Click Options ▼ .... Alt + O , F4

4. Select **Delete Summary From Document** ...... D

5. Click Yes .... Y

Print Document Summary

1. Select **File** menu .... `Alt`+`F`

2. Select **Document Summary** .... `Y`

3. Click `Options ▼` .... `Alt`+`O`, `F4`

4. Select **Print Summary** .... `P`

Save Document Summary as File

1. Select **File** menu .... `Alt`+`F`

2. Select **Document Summary** .... `Y`

3. Click `Options ▼` .... `Alt`+`O`, `F4`

4. Select **Save Summary As New Document** ...... `S`

5. Type filename .... *filename*

6. Click `  OK  ` .... `Enter`

Configure Document Summary Fields

Determines which fields appear in the document summary.

1. Select **File** menu .... `Alt`+`F`

2. Select **Document Summary** .... `Y`

3. Click `Configure...` .... `Alt`+`C`

continued...

Configure Document Summary Fields (continued)

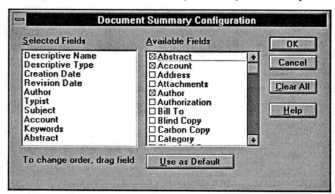

To indicate fields to include:

Select/deselect fields $\boxed{\text{Alt}}+\boxed{\text{A}}$, $\boxed{\uparrow}\boxed{\downarrow}$, $\boxed{\text{Space}}$ in **Available Fields** list.

To arrange fields:

Drag fields to new positions in **Selected Fields** list.

To use current settings as default document summary for all new documents:

Click $\boxed{\underline{\text{U}}\text{se as Default}}$ .... $\boxed{\text{Alt}}+\boxed{\text{U}}$

4. Click $\boxed{\quad \text{OK} \quad}$ .... $\boxed{\text{Enter}}$

Automate Summary with Preferences

Allows you to choose certain default settings for the document summary under Summary *and* Environment *Preferences. (See* PREFERENCES, *page 170, for more information.)*

DOCUMENT WINDOW

Switch to Open Document Window

1. Select **Window** menu .... `Alt`+`W`
2. Select document window number .... *number*

Reduce (Minimize) Window to Icon

Click `▾` .... `Alt`+`-`, `N`

Enlarge (Maximize) Document Window

Click `▴` .... `Alt`+`-`, `X`

Restore Maximized Document Window

Click `⬍` .... `Alt`+`-`, `R`

Arrange Document Windows

Drag window's title bar to desired location.

OR

1. Select **Window** menu .... `Alt`+`W`

2. Select **Cascade** ....`C`
    to arrange windows so they overlap, the title
    bar of each window remaining visible.

    OR

    Select **Tile** ....`T`
    to arrange windows so each is visible
    but doesn't overlap another.

DRAFT MODE

(See VIEW MODES, page 262.)

DRAG AND DROP

Lets you copy or move selected text with a mouse.

Copy/Move Text

Select text to copy/move.

To copy text:

a. Click 🗐 .... `Ctrl`+`C`

b. Click 📋 .... `Ctrl`+`V`
   to insert text.

To move text:

Drag selection to desired location.

ENDNOTES

(See FOOTNOTES AND ENDNOTES, page 66.)

ENVELOPE

Create Envelope

To create envelope for existing document:

Open desired document.

*NOTE: If you have more than one mailing address
          in a document, select desired one.*

1. Select **For̲mat** menu .... `Alt`+`R`

2. Select **En̲velope** .... `V`

continued.

Create Envelope (continued)

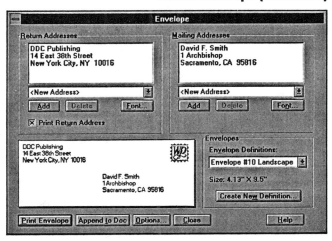

If an envelope definition does not exist, you are prompted to create one. (See Create Envelope Definition, page 53.)

To enter mailing address:

WordPerfect displays the address in the document. To accept it, skip to step d.

Select **<New Address>** .... `Tab`, `F4`, `↑` `↓`
from list.

OR

a. Type new address ....*address*

b. Click `Add` .... `Alt`+`D`
   to add new address for future use.

c. Highlight address................... `Alt`+`L`, `Y`
   and click `Delete` to delete existing address.

d. Click `Font...` .... `Alt`+`N`
   to change font, if desired.

continued...

Create Envelope (continued)

e. Select desired font option(s).

f. Click [**OK**] .... [Enter]

To enter return address:

WordPerfect displays the last return address used. To accept it, skip to step e.

a. Select **<New Address>** ..... [Tab], [F4], [↑][↓]

b. Type new address .... [Alt]+[R], *address*

c. Click [**Add**] .... [Alt]+[A]
    to add new address typed in step b.

d. Highlight address .... [Alt]+[E], [Y]
    and click [**Delete**] to delete existing address.

e. Click [**Font...**] .... [Alt]+[F]
    to change address font, if desired.

f. Select desired font option(s).

g. Click [**OK**] .... [Enter]

h. Select **Print Retu̲rn Address** .... [Alt]+[U]

To change envelope definition:

Select definition .... [Alt]+[V], [F4], [↑][↓]
from **En̲velope Definitions** list.

(See Create Envelope Definition, page 53, to create a new definition.)

continued

Create Envelope (continued)

To print envelope:

Click `Print Envelope` .... `Alt` + `P`

To insert envelope definition at end of document:

Click `Append to Doc` .... `Alt` + `T`

Create Envelope Definition

To display Envelope dialog box:

a. Select **Format** menu .... `Alt` + `R`

b. Select **Envelope** .... `V`

1. Click `Create New Definition...` .... `Alt` + `W`

2. Type definition .... *definition name*
   name in **Paper Name** box.

3. Select **Envelope** .... `Tab`, `F4`, `↑` `↓`
   in **Type** list.

4. Select desired size .... `Tab`, `F4`, `↑` `↓`
   from **Size** list.

5. Make selections from **Paper Location**, **Orientation**
   and **Text Adjustments**, if necessary.

6. Click `    OK    ` .... `Enter`

ENVIRONMENT SETTINGS

(See PREFERENCES, page 170.)

EQUATIONS

*The WordPerfect **Equation** feature illustrates equations; it does not calculate them.*

Equations appear in a graphic box. You can enter variables and select commands, symbols and mathematical functions from the equation palette within the Equation Editor.

Commands and symbols within Equation Editor are grouped by type into different sets.

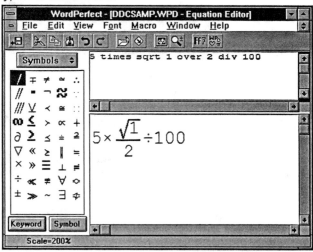

*The **Equation screen** displays three sections:*

- *The **Equation palette pop–up list** shows a list of commands and/or characters available within the active set of commands or symbols.*

- *The **Editing window** is where you type characters and commands.*

- *The **Display windows** shows you what the printed equation will look like.*

Create Equation

1. Position cursor where equation is to appear.

2. Select **Graphics** menu .... `Alt` + `G`

3. Select **Equation** .... `Q`

4. Type characters .... *characters* to appear outside or before symbol/command.

5. Select symbol/command .... *symbol* to insert from character/symbol/command set at left.

6. Click `Keyword` or `Symbol`

7. Type characters .... *characters* to appear inside or after symbol/command.

8. Click `⟳` .... `Ctrl` + `F3` on Equation Editor feature bar.

9. Click `↰` .... `Ctrl` + `F4` on Equation Editor feature bar.

> *EXAMPLE:* *The Editing window (upper right section) might contain the numbers and commands.*

```
156 LONGDIV 543234567
```

> *The Display window (lower right) after redisplaying appears.*

$$156\sqrt{543234567}$$

> *Selecting **Close** places the graphic display into the text as a graphic box which may then be edited as any graphic box. (See* **GRAPHICS**, *page 76.)*

Select Equation Palette

You may access the following palettes by clicking

| Commands ⬍ | *on the Equation screen (see above).*

PALETTE	WHAT IT DOES
<u>C</u>ommands	*Displays formatting commands represented by keywords.*
<u>L</u>arge	*Displays large and small mathematical, scientific, bracket and brace symbols.*
<u>S</u>ymbols	*Displays commonly used symbols.*
<u>G</u>reek	*Displays some upper– and lowercase Greek characters, as well as some variants.*
<u>A</u>rrows	*Displays arrow styles and hollow and solid figures such as triangles, squares and circles.*
S<u>e</u>ts	*Displays set symbols, relational operators and some Fraktur and hollow letters.*
<u>O</u>ther	*Displays diacritical marks (accents) and orientations of ellipses.*
<u>F</u>unction	*Displays mathematical functions, such as cos, sin and log.*

1. Select **Graphics** menu .... `Alt`+`G`

2. Select **Equation** .... `Q`

3. Click and hold | Commands ⬍ | at upper left side of screen.

The palette names listed above appear in pop–up list.

4. Highlight desired set.

5. Release mouse button.

Inline Equation

1. Select **Graphics** menu .... `Alt`+`G`
2. Select **Custom Box** ....`C`
3. Select **Inline Equation**.
4. Follow steps 4–9 of **Create Equation**, page 55.

Edit Equation

1. Double–click equation.
2. Make desired changes.
3. Click 🖅 .... `Ctrl`+`F4`

Equation Font

—FROM EQUATION EDITOR—

1. Click `FFF`
2. Choose desired options.
3. Click ▏‾‾OK‾‾▕ .... `Enter`

Save Equation as Text File

—FROM EQUATION EDITOR—

1. Press **F3** .... `F3`

*WordPerfect 6.1 appears in **Save File as Type** drop–down box.*

2. Type equation filename .... *filename.eqn*
   using .eqn extension
   in **Filename** text box.
3. Click ▏‾‾OK‾‾▕ .... `Enter`

Save Equation as Graphic File

—FROM EQUATION EDITOR—

1. Press **F3** .... `F3`

2. Type equation filename .... *filename.wpg*
   using .wpg extension
   in **Filename** text box.

   —IN SAVE FILE AS TYPE DROP–DOWN BOX—

3. Select **WordPerfect** .... `Alt`+`T`, `↑` `↓`
   Graphics 2.0.

4. Click `OK` .... `Enter`

Retrieve Equation Text File

1. Position cursor where equation is to appear.

2. Select **Graphics** menu .... `Alt`+`G`

3. Select **Equation** .... `Q`

4. Click ⬙ .... `Alt`+`F`, `I`

5. Specify path and select equation filename.

6. Click **Retrieve...** .... `Alt`+`R`

*The equation appears in the **Equation Editor** window. You can edit it before inserting it into the text.*

FAX

To fax from within WordPerfect, you must have a fax driver and a fax modem, and you must install a fax program. A fax driver is a program that translates file characters into signals that can be sent across telephone lines using a fax modem.

Faxing is very much like printing. Before you can print a document, you must tell WordPerfect what printer driver to use; before you can fax a document, you must tell WordPerfect what fax driver to use.

Setup/Select Fax Driver

1. Press **Ctrl+P** .... `Ctrl`+`P`
2. Click `Select...` .... `S`
3. Highlight desired fax driver ..... `Tab`, `F4`, `↑` `↓`
4. Click `Options ▼` .... `Alt`+`O`, `F4`
5. Select **Setup** .... `S`
6. Indicate how and where you wish to send your fax.
7. Click `OK` .... `Enter`
8. Click `Select` .... `Alt`+`S`

Send Fax

(See PRINT, page 171, for more information.)

1. Press **Ctrl+P** .... `Ctrl`+`P`
2. Confirm **Current Printer** is desired fax driver.

continued...

60

Send Fax (continued)

3. Choose desired print (fax) option(s).

4. Click [Print...] .... **Alt**+**P**
   to send fax.

   To cancel fax:
   (Cancels sending of current fax.)

   a. Press **Ctrl+P** .... **Ctrl**+**P**

   b. Click [Control...] .... **Alt**+**T**

   c. Select **Cancel** .... **Alt**+**C**

   To view fax activity:

   a. Press **Ctrl+P** .... **Ctrl**+**P**

   b. Click [Control...] .... **Alt**+**T**

   c. Select **Control** .... **Alt**+**T**

FIND

Find Word(s) or Code(s)

1. Press **F2** ....

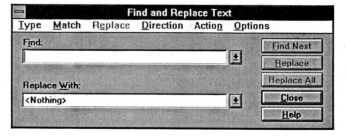

continued.

Find Word(s) or Code(s) (continued)

2. Type word(s)...*word(s)*
   to find.

   OR

   a. Select **Match** menu........................ `Alt`+`M`
      to find code.

   b. Select **Codes**...`O`

   c. Select desired code............................ `↑` `↓`

   d. Click `Insert` .... `Alt`+`I`

   e. Click `Close`

   OR

   a. Select **Type** menu .... `Alt`+`T`
      to find specific occurrence of code.

   b. Select **Specific Codes**..............................`S`

   c. Select desired code............................ `↑` `↓`

   d. Click `OK` ....`Enter`

3. Choose from the following options, if desired:

   To match whole words, case or typestyle:

   a. Select **Match** menu...................... `Alt`+`M`

   b. Choose desired option(s)....... `↑` `↓`, `Enter`

   To choose direction to search:

   a. Select **Direction** menu .... `Alt`+`D`

   b. Choose desired direction .... `↑` `↓`, `Enter`

continued...

Find Word(s) or Code(s) (continued)

To specify cursor placement for selected word(s)/code(s):

a. Select **Actio̲n** menu .... `Alt`+`N`

b. Choose desired position .... `↑` `↓`, `Enter`

4. Click `Find Next` .... `Enter`
   to find next occurrence.

5. Click `Close` .... `Esc`

Replace Text

1. Press **F2** .... `F2`

2. Complete steps 1–3 **Find Word(s) or Code(s),** page 60.

3. Type replacement ...... `Alt`+`W`, *replacement text* text in **Replace W̲ith** box.

4. Choose desired option:

   • `Find Next` .... `Enter`

     to find, but not replace, next occurrence.

   NOTE: *This option allows you to choose on a case by case basis if you wish to replace selected text.*

   • `R̲eplace` .... `Alt`+`R`

     to replace next occurrence.

   • `Replace A̲ll` .... `Alt`+`A`

   • `H̲elp` .... `Alt`+`H`

5. Click `Close` .... `Esc`

FLUSH RIGHT

NOTE: *Use **Right Justification** to align more than one line of text. (See **JUSTIFICATION**, page 114, for more information.)*

Flush Right Text

1. Place insertion point where alignment is to begin.

2. Press **Alt+F7**.......................... Alt + F7

Existing text is right aligned.

3. Type text.. *text*

Text is right aligned as it is typed.

4. Press **Enter**...................................... Enter
   to end right alignment.

Flush Right with Dot Leaders

1. Place insertion point where alignment is to begin.

2. Press **Alt+F7** twice .... Alt + F7, Alt + F7

3. Type text.. *text*

FONT

NOTES: *To display the Font Toolbar, shown below, select **Edit**, **Preferences**, **Toolbar**.*

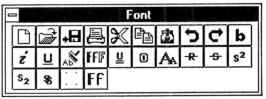

*Fonts displayed in the **Fonts** list box are those currently installed for the selected printer.*

Printer Initial Font

1. Press **Ctrl+P** .... `Ctrl` + `P`

2. Click `Select...` .... `S`

3. Click `Options ▼` .... `O`, `F4`

4. Select **Initial Font** .... `F`

5. Select desired font face, size and style.

   *NOTE: Not all font face selections have a variety of
   sizes and styles available.*

6. Click `OK` .... `Enter`

7. Click `Select` .... `Enter`

8. Click `Close` .... `Esc`

Document Initial Font

1. Select **Format** menu .... `Alt` + `R`

2. Select **Document** .... `D`

3. Select **Initial Font** .... `F`

4. Select desired font face, size and style.

5. Select **Set as Printer Initial Font** .... `Alt` + `E`
   check box to use settings as initial font for printer.

6. Click `OK` .... `Enter`

Change Base Font

1. Place insertion point where font change is to begin.
2. Click [Times New Roman (Printe▼] on power bar.
3 Select desired font face.
4 Click [12 pt ▼] on power bar.
5 Select desired font size.

Change Font Appearance, Position/Size

1. Select text to change, or place insertion point where font attributes are to begin.
2. Press **F9** .... [F9]

To change appearance:

NOTE: *These options may be chosen prior to typing text, or after text has already been typed.*

Select/deselect desired appearance attribute(s).

NOTE: *The three most popular appearance changes (bold face, italics and underline) are included on most Toolbars.*

*Hidden is only available when text is selected prior to going into the **Font** dialog box.*

To change positions:

Choose desired option.............[Alt]+[P], [↑][↓]
from **Position** list.

To change size:

Choose desired option.............[Alt]+[Z], [↑][↓]
from **Relative Size** list.

3. Click [OK] ....[Enter]

66

FOOTNOTES AND ENDNOTES

NOTE: *When you add and delete footnotes/endnotes, WordPerfect automatically renumbers existing notes, as necessary.*

Create Footnote/Endnote

1. Place insertion point where reference number should be placed.

2. Select **Insert** menu .... `Alt`+`I`

3. Select **Footnote** .... `F`
   OR

   Select **Endnote**.. `E`

4. Select **Create** .... `C`

5. Type note text...*text*

6. Click `Close` .... `Alt`+`Shift`+`C`

Edit Footnote/Endnote

1. Select **Insert** menu .... `Alt`+`I`

2. Select **Footnote** .... `F`
   OR

   Select **Endnote**.. `E`

3. Select **Edit** .... `E`

4. Enter desired note number .... *number*

continued

5. Click [OK] .... Enter

6. Edit note text.

7. Click [Close] .... Alt + Shift + C

Change Footnote Options

> *NOTE:* *You must turn on **Reveal Codes** before*
> *positioning footnote code. (See **Reveal***
> ***Codes**, page, 184, for more information.)*

1. Place insertion point before footnote to change.

2. Select **Insert** menu .... Alt + I

3. Select **Footnote** .... F

4. Select **Options** .... O

Footnote Options

Numbering Method
Method: [Numbers ▼]   Characters: [ ]
☐ Restart Numbering on Each Page

Edit Numbering Style
[In Text...] [In Note...]

Spacing Between Notes
Space: [0.167" ▲▼]

Position
○ Place Notes Below Text
◉ Place Notes at Bottom of Page

Continued Footnotes
Amount of Footnote to Keep Together: [0.500" ▲▼]
☐ Insert [continued...] Message

[OK]
[Cancel]
[Separator...]
[Help]

---

continued...

Change Footnote Options (continued)

To change numbering method:

Select desired numbering .... `F4`, `↑` `↓`
method in **Method** box.

*NOTE: If you select **Characters**, type desired characters in the **Characters** text box.*

To change line separating footnotes from text:

a. Select **Separator** .... `Alt`+`E`
b. Make desired changes.
c. Click ⌊ **OK** ⌉ .... `Enter`

To change space between notes:

a. Select **Space** .... `Alt`+`S`
b. Enter desired space .... *number*

To print (continued...) on last line of page and first line of next page:

Select **Insert (continued...)** .... `Alt`+`I`
Message check box.

To change location of printed footnotes:

Choose desired **Position** option.

To edit format for numbers in document text:

Click ⌊ **In Text...** ⌉ .... `Alt`+`T`

(See STYLES EDITOR, page, 206, for more information.)

continued.

Change Footnote Options (continued)

To indicate format for numbers in note:

Click | In Note... | .... Alt + N

To restart numbering on every page:

Select **Restart Numbering** .... Alt + R
on **Each Page** check box.

5. Click | OK | .... Enter

Change Endnote Options

1. Place insertion point before first endnote to change.

2. Select **Insert** menu .... Alt + I

3. Select **Endnote** .... E

4. Select **Options** .... O

To change numbering method:

Select desired numbering method.... F4, ↑ ↓

*NOTE: If you select **Characters**, type desired characters in **Characters** text box.*

continued...

Change Endnote Options (continued)

To change space between notes:

a. Select **Space** .... `Alt`+`S`

b. Enter desired space............................. *number*

To indicate minimum amount of space for endnote:

a. Select **Amount of Endnote** .... `Alt`+`A`
to Keep Together.

b. Enter desired space............................. *number*

To indicate format for numbers in document text:

Click `In Text...` .... `Alt`+`T`

To indicate format for numbers in note:

Click `In Note...` .... `Alt`+`N`

(See STYLES EDITOR, page 206, for more information.)

5. Click `OK` .... `Enter`

Position Endnotes Manually

1. Place insertion point where endnotes are to appear.

2. Select **Insert** menu .... `Alt`+`I`

3. Select **Endnote**.. `E`

4. Select **Placement** .... `P`

continued

Position Endnotes Manually (continued)

5. Select **Insert Endnotes** .... `I`
   at Insertion Point.

   OR

   Select **Insert Endnotes** .... `R`
   at Insertion Point
   and **Restart Numbering**.

6. Click ⟨ **OK** ⟩ .... `Enter`

Renumber Footnotes/Endnotes Manually

1. Place insertion point where endnotes are to appear.

2. Select **Insert** menu .... `Alt`+`I`

3. Select **Footnote** .... `F`

   OR

   Select **Endnote** .... `E`

4. Select **New Number** .... `N`

5. Select **Increase** .... `I`

   OR

   Select **Decrease** .... `D`

   OR

   Enter **New Number** .... `Alt`+`N`, *new number*

6. Click ⟨ **OK** ⟩ .... `Enter`

GENERATE

> *NOTE: Each time you generate, all items (TOC, Index, etc.) in the document are generated or regenerated.*

1. Press **Ctrl+F9** .... `Ctrl`+`F9`

   If you are using subdocuments *(see **MASTER DOCUMENT**, page 141)* **and do not want WordPerfect to generate and save them:**

   a. Click `Options...` .... `O`

   b. Deselect **Save Subdocuments** .... `S`

   If you have hypertext links in the document and wish to generate and save them:

   a. Click `Options...` .... `O`

   b. Select **Build Hypertext Links** .... `B`

2. Click `OK` twice .... `Enter`, `Enter`

GO TO

1. Press **Ctrl+G** .... Ctrl + G

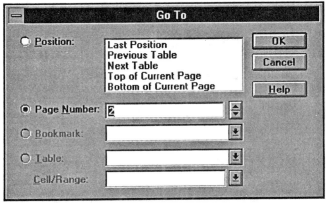

To go to top of specific page:
Enter desired page number .... *page number*

To go to specific position:

a. Select **Position** .... Alt + P

b. Select desired position....................... ↑ ↓
    from list.

To go to specific bookmark:

a. Select **Bookmark**............................... Alt + B

b   Select desired bookmark .... ↑ ↓
    from list.

To go to top of specific table:

a. Select **Table**....................................... Alt + T

b. Select desired table from list................ ↑ ↓

continued...

GO TO (continued)

To go to specific cell or range in table:

a. Select **Table** .... Alt + T

b. Select desired table from list.............. ↑ ↓

c. Select **Cell/Range** .... Alt + C

d. Type desired cell or range .... *cell* or *range*

2. Click [OK] .... Enter

GRAMMATIK

Proofread Document

1. Click 📖 ....Alt + Shift + F1
   on default Toolbar.

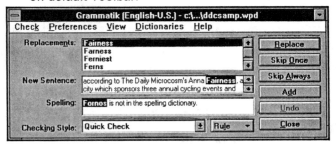

To change standard writing style:

a. Select **Preferences** menu.............. Alt + P

b. Select **Checking Styles** C

c. Select desired writing style .... ↑ ↓

d. Click [Select] .... Enter

continued.

Proofread Document (continued)

2. Choose desired options:

- | **Replace** | .... `Alt`+`R`

  to replace highlighted word/phrase
  with suggestion.

  *NOTE: If no suggestion is offered, you can replace
  manually.*

- | **Skip Once** | .... `Alt`+`O`

  to ignore highlighted word/phrase
  and go to next one.

- | **Skip Always** | .... `Alt`+`A`

  to ignore highlighted word/phrase (unless part
  of grammatical error) for rest of session.

- | **Add** | .... `Alt`+`D`

  to add word to dictionary.

- | **Undo** | .... `Alt`+`U`

  to reverse last action.

3. Click | **Close** | .... `Alt`+`C`
   to end grammar check.

Perform Analysis

1. Click 🔲 .... `Alt`+`Shift`+`F1`

2. Select **View** menu .... `Alt`+`V`

3. Select **Statistics** .... `S`

4. Click | **Close** | .... `Alt`+`C`
   to return to your document.

GRAPHICS—CREATE

NOTES: *For many of the procedures below, the*
Graphics Box feature bar must be displayed.
*If it is not displayed, press **Alt+G**, **E**.*

Graphics Box Style

*There are ten different **graphics box styles**, each altering the*
way graphics boxes appear on the screen and on printed
documents. The styles do not, however, determine what goes
inside a graphics box.

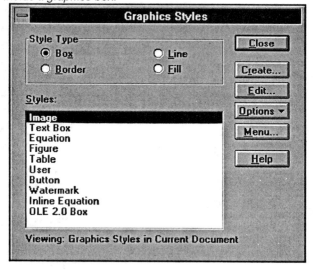

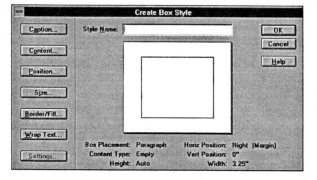

Graphics Box Feature Bar

The Graphics Box feature bar appears when a graphics box is added to a document. If the feature bar is not active, however, right-click and select Feature Bar.

> NOTE: Not all of the buttons shown above may not appear for all box styles.

Add Graphics Box to Document

Directs you to WordPerfect Draw or Equation Editor, depending on the box you create.

1. Place insertion point where graphics box is to appear.

2. Select **Graphics** menu .... `Alt`+`G`

3. Select **Custom Box** .... `C`

4. Select desired box style .... `↑` `↓`, `Enter`

   > NOTE: If a dialog box appears, make the appropriate selections and continue.

5. Click `Content...` .... `Shift`+`Alt`+`O`

6. Type or select .... `Alt`+`F`, *path/filename* path/filename.

7. Select desired option(s).

8. Click `OK` .... `Enter`

9. Click `Close` .... `Shift`+`Alt`+`C` to return to your document.

Retrieve Image into Document

1. Place insertion point where image is to appear.
2. Select **Graphics** menu .... `Alt`+`G`
3. Select **Image** .... `M`
4. Type/select .... *image path/filename*
   image path/filename.
5. Click `OK` .... `Enter`
6. Click `Close` .... `Shift`+`Alt`+`C`
   to return to your document.

Add Box Style to Menu

Image, Text and Equation graphics box styles already appear on the Graphics menu. Use this procedure to add other graphics box styles to the Graphics menu.

1. Select **Graphics** menu .... `Alt`+`G`
2. Select **Graphics Styles** .... `G`
3. Select **Box** .... `Alt`+`X`
4. Click `Menu...` .... `Alt`+`M`
5. Select/deselect desired **Items** .... `↑``↓`, `Space`
6. Click `OK` .... `Enter`
7. Click `Close` .... `Esc`
   to return to your document.

Change Box Style
—WITH GRAPHICS BOX FEATURE BAR ACTIVE—

1. Select graphics box.

2. Select `Style...` .... `Shift` + `Alt` + `T`

3. Select desired **Style**.............................. `↑` `↓`

4. Click `OK` .... `Enter`

5. Click `Close` .... `Shift` + `Alt` + `C`.

Delete Graphics Box

1. Select graphics box to delete.

2. Press **Delete** or **Backspace**.... `Del` or `Backspace`

Add/Edit Caption
—WITH GRAPHICS BOX FEATURE BAR ACTIVE—

1. Select graphics box.

2. Click `Caption...` .... `Shift` + `Alt` + `A`

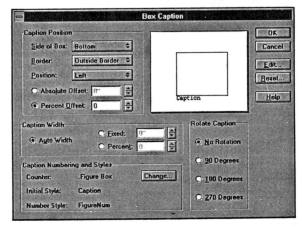

continued...

Add/Edit Caption (continued)

3. Choose desired option(s) in dialog box.

4. Click **Edit...** .... `Alt`+`E`

5. Type/edit caption text .... *caption text*

6. Click **Close** .... `Shift`+`Alt`+`C`
   to return to your document.

Delete Caption

1. Select graphics box.

2. Press **Shift+F11** .... `Shift`+`F11`

3. Right–click.

4. Click **Caption...** .... `Shift`+`Alt`+`A`

5. Click **Reset...** .... `Alt`+`R`
   to delete caption text and style.

6. Click **OK** twice .... `Enter`, `Enter`
   to delete caption.

7. Click **Close** .... `Shift`+`Alt`+`C`
   to return to your document.

Change Position of Caption

—WITH GRAPHICS BOX FEATURE BAR ACTIVE—

1. Select graphics box.

2. Click **Caption...** .... `Shift`+`Alt`+`A`

continued.

Change Position of Caption (continued)

To determine caption placement:

Select desired side .... F4, ↑ ↓, Enter
from list.

To determine caption/border placement:

a. Select **B**order .... Alt + B, F4

b. Select desired location .... ↑ ↓, Enter
from list.

To determine how caption is aligned to side of graphics box:

a. Select **P**osition .... Alt + P, F4

b. Select desired position........... ↑ ↓, Enter
from list.

To indicate distance to offset caption:

a. Select **Abso**l**u**te Offset.................. Alt + L

b. Enter distance .... Tab, *number*

To indicate percent to offset caption:

a. Select **Percent O**ffset................. Alt + O

b. Enter percent .... Tab, *number*

3. Click [OK] .... Enter

4. Click [**C**lose] .... Shift + Alt + C
to return to your document.

Rotate Caption
—WITH GRAPHICS BOX FEATURE BAR ACTIVE—

1. Select graphics box.
2. Click `Caption...` .... **Shift** + **Alt** + **A**
3. Choose desired angle of rotation to **Rotate Caption**.
4. Click `OK` .... **Enter**
5. Click `Close` .... **Shift** + **Alt** + **C**
   to return to your document.

Change Caption Numbering Style
—WITH GRAPHICS BOX FEATURE BAR ACTIVE—

1. Select graphics box.
2. Click `Caption...` .... **Shift** + **Alt** + **A**
3. Click `Change...` .... **Alt** + **G**
4. Choose one of the following options in the **Select Counter** dialog box:

COUNTERS	NUMBERING STYLE	APPEARANCE
<None>		
Equation Box	equation	(1)
Figure Box	figure	Figure 1
Table Box	table	Table 1
Text Box	text	1
User Box	user	1

NOTE: You may also create your own style. (See **STYLES**, *page 206, for more information.)*

continued

5. Click `Select` .... `Enter`

6. Click `OK`

7. Click `Close` .... `Shift`+`Alt`+`C`.

Adjust Caption Width

—WITH GRAPHICS BOX FEATURE BAR ACTIVE—

1. Select graphics box.

2. Click `Caption...` .... `Shift`+`Alt`+`A`

   To adjust width based on caption length and box size:

   Select **Auto Width** .... `Alt`+`U`

   To specify fixed measurement (not greater than width or height of box):

   a. Select **Fixed** .... `Alt`+`F`

   b. Enter measurement .... `Tab`, *number*

   To specify measurement based on percentage of box size:

   a. Select **Percent** .... `Alt`+`T`

   b. Enter percentage...................... `Tab`, *number*

3. Click `OK` .... `Enter`

4. Click `Close` .... `Shift`+`Alt`+`C`
   to return to your document.

GRAPHICS—EDIT

*NOTE: For all the procedures below, the Graphics Box feature bar must be displayed. If it is not displayed, right–click and press **F**, **W**.*

Display Image Tools

—WITH GRAPHICS BOX FEATURE BAR ACTIVE—

Click ⌐Tools¬ .... **Shift** + **Alt** + **L**

NOTE: To learn the function of each image tool, place the cursor on the desired icon; a description appears in the title bar.

Close Image Tools

Click ⌐Tools¬ .... **Shift** + **Alt** + **L**

Double–click ⊟

OR

Click outside graphics box to return to your document.

Rotate Image

—WITH GRAPHICS BOX FEATURE BAR ACTIVE—

1. Select graphics box.

2. Click ⌐Tools¬ .... **Shift** + **Alt** + **L**

continued.

3. Click 🔄

4. Drag ✪ to new location.

5. Drag 🔃 in correct direction.

6. Click outside graphics box to return to document.

Specify Degree of Rotation

—WITH GRAPHICS BOX FEATURE ACTIVE—

1. Select graphics box.

2. Click 【 Tools 】.............................. Shift + Alt + L

3. Click 🔳

4. Select **Rotate Image** ....O

5. Enter **Amount** .... Tab , *degree of rotation*

   NOTE: *For clockwise, use negative numbers. For counter–clockwise, use positive numbers.*

6. Click 【 OK 】 .... Enter

7. Click outside graphics box to return to document.

Invert Color Image

—WITH GRAPHICS BOX FEATURE BAR ACTIVE—

1. Select graphics box.

2. Click 【 Tools 】.............................. Shift + Alt + L

3. Click 🔳

4. Click outside graphics box to return to document.

86

Change Image to Black/White
—WITH GRAPHICS BOX FEATURE BAR ACTIVE—

1. Select graphics box.
2. Click `Tools` .... **Shift** + **Alt** + **L**
3. Click 🖼
4. Select desired **Black & White** check box on **Threshold** palette.
5. Click outside graphics box to return to document.

Specify Image Contrast
—WITH GRAPHICS BOX FEATURE BAR ACTIVE—

1. Select graphics box.
2. Click `Tools` .... **Shift** + **Alt** + **L**
3. Click ◐
4. Select desired **Contrast**.
5. Click outside graphics box to return to document.

Specify Image Brightness
—WITH GRAPHICS BOX FEATURE BAR ACTIVE—

1. Select graphics box.
2. Click `Tools` .... **Shift** + **Alt** + **L**
3. Click ☼
4. Select desired **Brightness**.
5. Click outside graphics box to return to document.

Create Mirror Image
—WITH GRAPHICS BOX FEATURE BAR ACTIVE—

1. Select graphics box.
2. Click `Tools` .... `Shift`+`Alt`+`L`
3. Click `▶◀`
   OR
   Click `≛`
4. Click outside graphics box to return to document.

Scale Image
—WITH GRAPHICS BOX FEATURE BAR ACTIVE—

1. Select graphics box.
2. Click `Tools` .... `Shift`+`Alt`+`L`
3. Click `🔍`
4. Click `↖` and `↕` from pop–up list.
5. Drag scroll box to scale image.
6. Click outside graphics box to return to document.

Replace Image
—WITH GRAPHICS BOX FEATURE BAR ACTIVE—

1. Select graphics box.
2. Click `Content...` .... `Shift`+`Alt`+`O`

continued…

Replace Image (continued)

3. Type new **Filename**........................ **F**, *filename*

    OR

    Click 🖻 and select desired file to replace.

4. Specify different image.................. *different image*

5. Click [**OK**   ] three times................. **Enter**

6. Click outside graphics box to return to document.

Customize Graphics Box Border

   —WITH GRAPHICS BOX FEATURE BAR ACTIVE—

1. Select graphics box.

2. Click [Border/Fill...]........................ **Shift**+**Alt**+**B**

3. Click [**C**ustomize Style...] .... **C**

4. Choose desired options to customize style, color, corners, etc.

5. Click [**OK**   ] twice .... **Enter**, **Enter**

6. Click outside graphics box to return to document.

Move Between Images

   —WITH GRAPHICS BOX FEATURE BAR ACTIVE—

   To move to next graphics box:

   Click [**N**ext]........................ **Shift**+**Alt**+**N**

   To move to previous graphics box:

   Click [P**r**ev]........................ **Shift**+**Alt**+**R**

Anchor Types

When you create a graphics box, it is attached (anchored) to something. The default anchoring types are listed below.

STYLE DEFAULT:	ANCHOR TYPE:
Figure	Paragraph
Text	Paragraph
Equation	Paragraph
Table	Paragraph
User	Paragraph
Inline Equation	Character

Anchor Graphics Box to Text

You should be aware of the following anchoring characteristics:

Page Anchor — *Box stays with page, even if information is added and/or deleted.*

Paragraph Anchor — *Box stays with paragraph. If information is added to push paragraph to next page, box moves to next page.*

Character Anchor — *Box is treated just like a single character of text.*

Change Text Flow Around Graphics Box

—WITH GRAPHICS BOX FEATURE BAR ACTIVE—

1. Select graphics box.

2. Click Wrap... ....

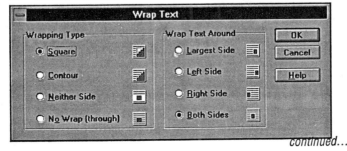

continued...

Change Text Flow Around Graphics Box (continued)

3. Select desired **Wrapping Type** option.

    *NOTE: Use **Contour** to eliminate unwanted white
    space around a graphic.*

4. Select desired **Wrap Text Around** option.

    *NOTE: Use **Largest Side** to make text flow on side
    of graphic with most white space.*

5. Click | **OK** | .... **Enter**

6. Click | **Close** | .... **Shift** + **Alt** + **C**
    to return to your document.

Move Box

—WITH GRAPHICS BOX FEATURE BAR ACTIVE—

1. Select graphics box.

2. Drag to new location.

    *CAUTION: Do not drag by handles on corners or
    sides.*

    OR

    a. Click **Position...** .... **Shift** + **Alt** + **P**

    b. Choose desired options.

    If you select [Page Anchor]:

    a. Select **Horizontal Place** .... **L**

    b. Enter horizontal place................**Tab**, *number*

    c. Select **Vertical Place** .... **Alt** + **C**

    d. Enter vertical measurement................ *number*

continued.

Move Box (continued)

If you select [Paragraph Anchor]:

a. Select **Horizontal Place** ....

b. Enter horizontal place .... *number*

c. Select **Vertical Place** ....

d. Enter vertical measurement .... *number*

If you select [Character Anchor]:
Select desired box position.

3. Click | OK | .... Enter

4. Click | Close | .... Shift + Alt + C

Size Box

—WITH GRAPHICS BOX FEATURE BAR ACTIVE—

1. Select graphics box.

2. Drag by handles to reduce or enlarge.

   OR

   a. Select graphics box.

   b. Click | Size... | .... Shift + Alt + S

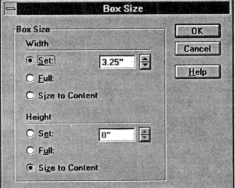

continued...

Size Box (continued)

Width

To specify exact measurement:

Enter width measurement...............`Tab`, *number*

To specify width from left to right margins (or width of column):

Select **F**ull .... `F`

To adjust width automatically to box contents:

Select S**i**ze to Content .... `I`

Height

To specify exact measurement:

a. Select S**e**t.................................... `Alt`+`E`
b. Enter height measurement .... *number*

To specify height from top to bottom margins:

Select F**u**ll .... `U`

To adjust height automatically to box contents:

Select Si**z**e to Content .... `Z`

3. Click `  OK  ` .... `Enter`

4. Click `  Close  ` .... `Shift`+`Alt`+`C`
   to return to your document.

Distort Image

—WITH GRAPHICS BOX FEATURE BAR ACTIVE—

1. Select graphics box.

continued.

Distort Image (continued)

2. Click [Content...] .... Shift + Alt + O

3. Select **Preserve Image** .... Alt + P
   Width/Height Ratio check box.

4. Complete **Size Box** procedure, above, to resize box.

5. Click [OK] .... Enter

6. Click [Close] .... Shift + Alt + C
   to return to your document.

Predefined Lines

Options for the predefined lines appear below.

OPTION:	HORIZONTAL LINE:	VERTICAL LINE:
Style	Single	Single
Type	Horizontal	Vertical
Horizontal Position	Full	Left
Vertical Position	Baseline	Full
Length	6.5"	9.0"
Space Above Line	0"	N/A
Space Below Line	0"	N/A
Border Offset	N/A	0"
Line Color	Black	Black
Line Thickness	0.012"	0.012"

Add Horizontal/Vertical Predefined Lines

1. Place insertion point where you wish to add line.

2. Click [↔] .... Ctrl + F11
   on Graphics Toolbar for horizontal line.

   OR

   Click [⇅] .... Shift + Ctrl + F11
   for vertical line.

Create Custom Lines

1. Place insertion point on page/line where line is to appear.

2. Click ⟦↩⟧ .... `Alt`+`G`, `L`

3. Choose desired options as described below.

OPTION:	KEYSTROKES:	ACTION:
Line Style	`Alt`+`L`, `Tab`, `F4`	Gives you choice of different line styles.
Line Type	`Alt`+`O` `Alt`+`V`	Gives you choice of horizontal or vertical.
Horizontal Position	`Alt`+`R`, `F4`	Sets horizontal position.
Vertical Position	`Alt`+`E`, `F4`	Sets vertical position.
Length	`Alt`+`N`	Lets you set line length.
Spacing	`Alt`+`A` `Alt`+`B`	Specifies spacing above and below line.
Change Color	`Alt`+`I`	Changes line color.
Change Thickness	`Alt`+`T`	Changes line thickness.
Line Styles	`Alt`+`Y`	Selects line styles.

4. Click ⟦ OK ⟧ .... `Enter`

Delete Graphics Line

1. Click line to delete.

A four-headed arrow appears [✥].

2. Press **Delete** or **Backspace**.... [Del] or [Backspace]

Edit Line

1. Click line to edit.

2. Edit as usual.

OR
Drag to new location.

OR
Drag one of sizing handles on the lines to shorten/lengthen line.
Mouse pointer should be a four-headed arrow.

HARD SPACE

Inserts a special space character, keeping two words together on a line. If the second word does not fit on a line, however, both words wrap to next line or page.

1. Place insertion point where you would like to insert a hard space.

2. Delete existing space, if necessary .... [Del]

3. Select **Format** menu .... [Alt]+[R]

4. Select **Line** .... [L]

5. Select **Other Codes** .... [O]

6. Select **Hard Space [HSpace]** .... [Alt]+[P]

7. Click [**Insert**] .... [Enter]

96

HEADERS AND FOOTERS

Create Header/Footer

> NOTE: This procedure is designed for Page or
> Two Page mode.

1. Place insertion point in first paragraph on first page
   where header or footer is to appear.

2. Select **Format** menu .... **Alt**+**R**

3. Select **Header/Footer** .... **H**

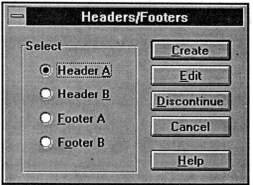

4. Choose desired option.

5. Click **Create** .... **C**

The Header/Footer feature bar appears.

6. Type and format header/footer ...*header/footer text*
   text as desired.

7. Click **Close** .... **Shift**+**Alt**+**C**
   to return to your document.

Edit Header/Footer

> *NOTE: This procedure is designed for Page or Two Page mode.*

1. Place insertion point on page where header/footer appears.

2. Select **Format** menu ....

3. Select **Header/Footer** .... ⊞

4. Choose header/footer to edit.

5. Click [**Edit**] .... Ⓔ

The Header/Footer feature bar appears.

To adjust position:

a. Click [Distance...] ....

b. Select desired distance between text and header.

c. Click [**OK**] .... Enter

6. Edit text.

To add page number, section number, etc., to header/footer:

a. Click [Number ▼] ....

b. Select desired option.

(See PAGE NUMBERING, page 160, for more information.)

continued...

Edit Header/Footer (continued)

To add line to header/footer:

Click ⟨↔⟩ .... `Ctrl`+`F11`
on Graphics Toolbar for horizontal line

OR

Click ⟨↕⟩ .... `Shift`+`Ctrl`+`F11`
on Graphics Toolbar for vertical line.

*(See Add Horizontal/Vertical Predefined Lines, page 93,
to edit line.)*

NOTE: You can also use graphics features.

7. Click ⟨ **Close** ⟩ .... `Shift`+`Alt`+`C`
to return to your document.

Discontinue Header/Footer

1. Complete steps 1–4, **Edit Header/Footer**, page 97.

2. Click ⟨Discontinue⟩ .... `Alt`+`D`

Delete Header/Footer

1. Use **Find** feature to locate code to delete.

(See FIND, page 60.)

OR

Use **Reveal Codes** feature to locate code to delete.

(See REVEAL CODES, page 184.)

2. Press **Delete** or **Backspace**... `Del` or `Backspace`

OR

Drag code to delete out of **Reveal Codes** window.

Adjust Distance Below Header/Above Footer

> *NOTE:* *This procedure is designed for Page or Two Page mode.*

1. Complete steps 1–5, **Edit Header/Footer**, page 97.

—WITH HEADER/FOOTER FEATURE BAR ACTIVE—

2. Click [Distance...] .... `Shift`+`Alt`+`D`

3. Enter **Distance Between Text** .... *number* **and Header.**

4. Click [OK] .... `Enter`

5. Click [C**l**ose] .... `Shift`+`Alt`+`C` to return to your document.

Move Quickly Between Headers/Footers

To move to next or previous header/footer quickly:

—WITH HEADER/FOOTER FEATURE BAR ACTIVE—

Click [Next] .... `Shift`+`Alt`+`N`

or [Previous] .... `Shift`+`Alt`+`P`

100

HIDE BARS

1. Press **Shift+Alt+F5** .... Shift + Alt + F5

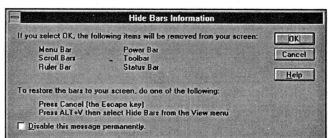

To disable dialog box:

Select **Disable this Message** .... Alt + D
Permanently check box.

2. Click [OK] .... Enter

To redisplay screen elements:
Repeat steps 1–2, above.

HYPERTEXT

Hypertext is a feature for online documents. It lets you link a part of your document to another part of the same document. You can also use it to link a part of your document to a different document or macro.

When you link to a document, you link to an existing bookmark. The bookmark can be in the current document or another document. (See BOOKMARKS, page 9, for more information.)

Hypertext links can be in two basic styles: highlighted words, phrases, or objects and hypertext buttons. When you create hypertext links, you use the Hypertext feature bar (see page 101).

Create Hypertext Link

To display Hypertext feature bar:

a. Select **Tools** menu .... `Alt`+`T`

b. Select **Hypertext** .... `H`

The Hypertext feature bar appears.

| `?` | `Perform` | `Back` | `Next` | `Previous` | `Create...` | `Edit...` | `Delete` | `Deactivate` | `Style...` | `Close` |

1. Select words or symbols to use as link.

2. Click `Create...` .... `Shift`+`Alt`+`T`

3. Choose desired option(s).

   To indicate how you want link to appear:
   Select **Text** or **Button**.

4. Type bookmark or document name .... *name*

5. Click `OK` .... `Enter`

6. Click `Close` .... `Shift`+`Alt`+`C`
   to return to your document.

Use Link

Click highlighted text or button.

   —WITH HYPERTEXT FEATURE BAR ACTIVE—

   To jump when link is inactive:

   Click `Perform` .... `Shift`+`Alt`+`R`

   To move from bookmark back to link:

   Click `Back...` .... `Shift`+`Alt`+`B`

continued...

Use Link (continued)

> **To move to next link:**
>
> Click Next .... Shift + Alt + N
>
> **To move to previous link:**
>
> Click Previous .... Shift + Alt + P

Edit Link

> *—WITH HYPERTEXT FEATURE BAR ACTIVE—*
>
> **To turn off links:**
>
> Click Deactivate .... Shift + Alt + A

1. Place insertion point on button.

   OR

   Place insertion point within hypertext link.

2. Click Edit... .... Shift + Alt + E

   *NOTE: If the insertion point is not on a link when you select **Edit**, WordPerfect displays the previous link for you to edit. If links have not been placed earlier in the document, WordPerfect will display the next link.*

3. Edit link, as desired.

4. Click OK .... Enter

Add Text to Link Button

> *—WITH HYPERTEXT FEATURE BAR ACTIVE—*

1. Place pointer over link button.

2. Right–click.

continued.

Add Text to Link Button (continued)

3. Select **Edit Text** .... 🅴

4. Type desired text .... *text*

5. Click [**Close**] .... Shift + Alt + C
to return to your document.

Delete Link

—WITH HYPERTEXT FEATURE BAR ACTIVE—

To turn off links:

Click [Deactivate] .... Shift + Alt + A

*Deactivate button changes to **Activate** button.*

1. Place insertion point on button.

2. Press **Delete** .... Del

Edit Hypertext Style

Changes how all hypertext links appear in the current document. This procedure does not, however, change the appearance of link buttons.

> *NOTE: Links are underlined in green by default.*

> *—WITH HYPERTEXT FEATURE BAR ACTIVE—*

1. Click [Style...] .... Shift + Alt + S

2. Select desired settings in **Styles Editor** dialog box.

(See STYLES, page 206, for more information.)

3. Click [**OK**] .... Enter

4. Click [**Close**] .... Shift + Alt + C
to return to your document.

HYPHENATION

Turn Hyphenation On/Off

1. Place insertion point where hyphenation is to begin/end.

2. Select **For_mat** menu .... **Alt** + **R**

3. Select **Line** .... **L**

4. Select **Hyphenation** .... **E**

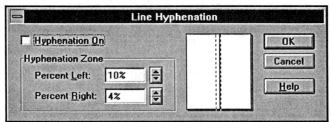

5. Select/deselect **Hyphenation On** check box ..... **O**

6. Click **OK** .... **Enter**

The word requiring hyphenation is displayed with a suggested hyphen position.

7. Select desired hyphen position .... **←** **→** in **Position Hyphen** dialog box.

   *NOTE: WordPerfect limits hyphen position by the hyphenation zone (see **Set Hyphenation Zone**, below).*

8. Choose desired option.

   *NOTES: A **Soft Hyphen** divides a word with a hyphen where the word crosses the right margin.*

continued

Turn Hyphenation On/Off (continued)

*A **Hyphenation Soft Return** divides a word with a space instead of a hyphen where the word crosses the right margin.*

*WordPerfect inserts a **[Hyph Ign Wrd]** code to prevent word from restarting hyphenation process.*

9. Press **Enter** .... `Enter`
   when hyphen is in desired location.

10. Repeat steps above for each word to hyphenate.

Set Hyphenation Zone

1. Place insertion point where setting is to begin.

2. Select **For̲mat** menu .... `Alt`+`R`

3. Select **L̲ine** .... `L`

4. Select **Hyph̲enation** .... `E`

5. Select **Percent L̲eft** text box .... `L`

6. Enter percentage .... *number*

7. Select **Percent R̲ight** text box .... `Alt`+`R`

8. Enter percentage .... *number*

   NOTE: Decrease the percentages in each text box to hyphenate more words. These numbers represent a percentage of the line length to the left or right of the right margin.

9. Select **Hyphenation O̲n** check box .... `Alt`+`O`

10. Click ⎡ **Insert** ⎤ .... `Enter`

Set Hyphenation Preferences
(See PREFERENCES, page 170.)

Insert Special Hyphenation Codes

1. Place insertion point where code is to appear.

2. Select **Fo_r_mat** menu .... `Alt`+`R`

3. Select **_L_ine**.. `L`

4. Select **_O_ther Codes**.................................... `O`

5. Choose desired **Hyphenation Codes** options.

6. Click `Insert` .... `Enter`

Cancel Hyphenation on Word

1. Place insertion point on first letter of word.

2. Select **Fo_r_mat** menu .... `Alt`+`R`

3. Select **_L_ine**.. `L`

4. Select **_O_ther Codes**.................................... `O`

5. Select **Cancel Hyphenation** .... `W`
   of _W_ord [Cancel Hyph].

6. Click `Insert` .... `Enter`

7. Delete existing hyphen in word, if necessary.

INDENT

1. Place insertion point where indent is to begin.

   NOTE: The buttons shown below are found on the
   Format Toolbar.

   To indent left side of paragraph to next tab stop:

   Click ⊞ .... `F7`

   To indent all lines (except first) to next tab stop:

   Click ⊞ .... `Ctrl`+`F7`

   To indent left and right side one tab stop:

   Click ⊞ .... `Ctrl`+`Shift`+`F7`

   NOTE: To align only the first line of text with the
   previous tab stop, select **Fo_r_mat**,
   ***P_a_ragraph, Back _T_ab**.

2. Type text... *text*

3. Press **Enter**... `Enter`
   to end paragraph and indenting.

INDEX

To create an index, you must complete the following three
steps:

   1.   Create a concordance file and/or mark items to
   include in index.

   2.   Define the index style and location.

   3.   Generate the index.

When you mark items for an index and define an index, the
Index feature bar appears at the top of the screen. It contains
text boxes and buttons needed to create an index.

continued…

INDEX (continued)

| ? Heading: | ± Subheading: | ± | Mark | Define... | Close | Generate... |

For most of the procedures below, the Index feature bar must be active:

Click 📝 .... Alt + T , X
on Generate Toolbar.

Create Concordance File

A concordance file is a list of items WordPerfect uses to generate an index. WordPerfect searches your document for entries in the concordance file and inserts the entry and its page number in the index.

1. Open new document.

2. Type entry for index.............................. *index entry*

3. Press **Enter** .... Enter

4. Repeat steps 2–3 for each entry.

5. Save and name the document.

6. Sort the document *(see **SORT**, page 194).*

7. Save the document.

Mark Index Entries

1. Open document to index.

2. Click 📝 .... Alt + T , X
on Generate Toolbar.

The Index feature bar appears.

To create heading/subheading:

a. Select or type word(s)................................. *text*
to include in index.

Mark Index Entries (continued)

continued

b. Click **H<u>e</u>ading** .... `Shift`+`Alt`+`E`

and **<u>S</u>ubheading** .... `Shift`+`Alt`+`S`

c. Click ⌊ <u>M</u>ark ⌋ .... `Shift`+`Alt`+`M`

> *NOTE:* *Heading/subheading text does not have to match selected word(s). You can type any information. The page number matches the location of the selected text.*

3. Repeat step 2 until all headings/subheadings are marked.

> *NOTE:* *After headings/subheadings are created, you must choose them again from the box (without retyping) to place additional entries under the same heading.*

To define index now:
Complete **Define Index**, below.

To return to document:
Click ⌊ **<u>C</u>lose** ⌋ .... `Alt`+`C`

Define Index

—WITH INDEX FEATURE BAR ACTIVE—

1. Place insertion point where index is to appear.

2. Type title.. *title*
if desired (e.g., INDEX).

3. Press **Enter**.. `Enter`
for spacing, as desired.

4. Click ⌊ <u>D</u>efine... ⌋ .... `Shift`+`Alt`+`D`

continued...

Define Index (continued)

To choose page numbering position:

a. Select **Position**.

b. Choose desired option .... `F4`, `↑` `↓`

To change page numbering format:

a. Click `Page Numbering...` .... `Alt`+`N`

b. Select **Document Page** .... `Alt`+`D`
   Number Format to return
   to document page number format.

   OR

   Select **User–Defined Page** .... `Alt`+`U`
   Number Format, if desired.

   OR

   Click `Insert ▾` .... `Alt`+`I`, `F4`
   for more page number format options.

c. Click `OK` .... `Enter`

To see each number printed (e.g., 20, 21, 22) instead of combined (e.g., 20–22):

Deselect **Use Dash to Show** .... `Alt`+`U`
Consecutive Pages check box.

To change heading and subheading style:

a. Click `Change...` .... `Alt`+`C`

b. Make desired changes.

c. Click `OK` .... `Enter`

continue

Define Index (continued)

If you are using a concordance file:

Type filename .... [Alt]+[F], *filename*
in **Filename** box.

5. Click [OK] .... [Enter]

<<Index will generate here>> appears beneath your title.

Generate Index

—FROM GENERATE TOOLBAR/FEATURE BAR—

Click [⟁] .... [Shift]+[Alt]+[G], [Enter]

Index appears. (See GENERATE, page 72, for more information.)

INITIAL CODES STYLE

(See TEMPLATES, page 250, for more information.)

Create Initial Codes Style

*NOTES: This procedure uses the **Styles Editor**.*

This procedure can be completed at any time. It can also be completed from anywhere in a WordPerfect document.

1 Select **Format** menu .... [Alt]+[R]

2. Select **Document** .... [D]

3. Select **Initial Codes Style** .... [S]

4. Make desired selections from the menus in the **Styles Editor** dialog box.

5. Click [OK] .... [Enter]

Edit Initial Codes Style

1. Select **Format** menu .... **Alt**+**R**

2. Select **Document** .... **D**

3. Select **Initial Codes Style** .... **S**

4. Type description .... **Alt**+**D**, *description*
   in **Description** text box.

   To add codes:
   a. Place insertion point where codes are to
      appear.

   b. Select desired options from menus in **Styles
      Editor**.

   To delete codes:
   Drag codes out of **Styles Editor**.

   OR

   a. Place insertion point to left of code(s) to
      delete.

   b. Press **Delete** .... **Del**

5. Click [**OK**] .... **Enter**

INSERT HARD RETURNS/TABS

1. Place cursor where hard return or tab is to appear.

2. Choose one of the following options:

   To insert hard return [HRt]:

   Press **Shift+Enter** .... **Shift**+**Enter**

continued

INSERT HARD RETURNS/TABS (continued)

To insert hard tab:

a. Select Fo_r_mat .... Alt + R

b. Select _L_ine L

c. Select _O_ther Codes .... O

d. Select _L_eft [Hd Left Tab] L

INITIAL FONT

(See FONT, page 63.)

INSERTION POINT MOVEMENT

> *NOTE:* *If you use the scroll bars, you must click the desired position in your document, otherwise, the insertion point stays in the same place.*

Move Insertion Point

(See GO TO, page 73, for more information.)

Move mouse until insertion point is in correct location and click.

OR

> *NOTE:* *The information below applies only to the default keyboard (CUA). (See **KEYBOARD**, page 117, for more information.)*

TO MOVE:	PRESS:
Left/Right One Character	← →
Left/Right One Word	Ctrl + ← / →
Up/Down One Line	↑ ↓
Beginning of Line	Home

continued…

114

Move Insertion Point (continued)

TO MOVE: **PRESS:**

Up/Down One Paragraph...................... `Ctrl` + `↑` / `↓`

Previous/Next Column....................... `Alt` + `←` / `→`

Top/Bottom of Screen........................... `Page Up` or `Page Down`
(then up/down one screen at a time)

First Line Previous/.......................... `Alt` + `Page Up` / `Page Down`
Next Page

Beginning of Document.......................... `Ctrl` + `Home`
(after initial style code)

End of Document .... `Ctrl` + `End`
(after formatting codes)

JUSTIFICATION

> *NOTES: Text is left justified, by default.*
>
> *To access Format Toolbar, select **Edit**,
> **Preferences**, **Toolbar** and click **Select**
> button.*

1. Select text to justify, or place insertion point where justification is to begin.

2. Choose one of the following Format Toolbar buttons:

continued.

- ⊟ .... `Ctrl` + `L`
- ⊟ .... `Ctrl` + `E`
- ⊟ .... `Ctrl` + `R`
- ⊟ .... `Ctrl` + `J`

NOTE: To justify all, select **For̲mat**, **J̲ustification**,
A̲ll, or click ⊟

KEEP TEXT TOGETHER

*Gives you access to three important features: Widow/Orphan,
Block Protect and Conditional End of Page.*

Widow/Orphan *prevents single lines from appearing at the
bottom or top of a page.*

Block Protect *keeps selected text together, not allowing it to
be divided between two pages. This feature is often used to
keep a table together, for example.*

Conditional End of Page, *which is often used to keep a
heading and the first lines of the first paragraph (after the
heading) together, keeps a specified number of lines together
on a page.*

1. Place insertion point where you want to keep text
together.

2. Click ⊟ on Page Toolbar.

   OR

   a. Select **For̲mat** .... `Alt` + `R`

   b. Select **P̲age** .... `P`

continued...

c. Select **K**eep Text Together...................... `K`

d. Select **P**revent the first .... `P`
and last lines of paragraphs from being
separated across pages check box.

OR

Select **K**eep selected text together........... `K`
on same page check box.

OR

i   Select **N**umber of lines....................... `N`
to keep together check box.

ii Type number of lines .... *number*
to keep together.

3. Click [**OK**] .... `Enter`

KERN TEXT

Turn Automatic Kerning On/Off

1. Place insertion point where kerning is to begin/end,
or select desired text.

2. Select **Fo**r**mat** menu .... `Alt`+`R`

3. Select **T**ypesetting.................................. `T`

4. Select **W**ord/Letter Spacing...................... `W`

5. Select/deselect **A**utomatic Kerning .... `A`

6. Click [**OK**] .... `Enter`

Manually Kern Text

1. Place insertion point between letters to kern.

   NOTE: WordPerfect will only kern the letters on either side of the insertion point.

2. Select **Fo_r_mat** menu .... `Alt`+`R`

3. Select **_T_ypesetting** .... `T`

4. Select **_M_anual Kerning** .... `M`

5. Select desired units .... `Alt`+`U`, `F4`, `↑``↓`
   of measure from pop–up list.

6. Enter **_A_mount** .... `Alt`+`A`, *number*
   to adjust in text box.

   NOTE: A negative number decreases the space between the two letters; a positive number increases it.

7. Click `  OK  ` .... `Enter`

KEYBOARD

Keyboard preferences let you select, define and create/edit the keyboard definition you use with WordPerfect. Three predefined keyboards come with WordPerfect: Equation Editor, WPDOS Compatible, and WPWin 6.1. (See PREFERENCES, page 170, for more information.)

   NOTE: You cannot edit the three predefined keyboards.

KICKOFF

Starts an application or opens a file automatically. KickOff is also designed to update QuickFinder indexes. (See QUICKFINDER, page 178.)

Setup KickOff

1. Exit WordPerfect 6.1 for Windows.

    —FROM WORDPERFECT GROUP—

2. Click KickOff

3. Click **Setup...** ....**Alt**+**S**

    To run KickOff as icon from Program Manager:

    Select **Start KickOff minimized** ....**Alt**+**S**
    check box.

    To remove a KickOff event after it is completed:

    Select **Remove events** ....**Alt**+**R**
    upon completion check box.

    NOTE: An event is considered completed if it was executed and you have not specified a repeat interval.

    To disable event(s) that are past date and time (with no specified interval) on startup of next KickOff:

    Select **Disable old events**...................**Alt**+**D**
    on startup check box.

continued.

To continue launching events after an error during a launch:

Select **W**rite launch errors .... `Alt`+`W`
to a log file check box.

NOTE: *Error messages are saved in the log file*
KICKOFF.LOG.

4. Click `    OK    ` .... `Enter`

5. Click `    Close    ` .... `Esc`

Add KickOff Event

1. Exit WordPerfect for Windows 6.1.

—FROM WORDPERFECT GROUP—

2. Click KickOff

3. Click `    Add...    ` .... `Alt`+`A`

The Edit/Add dialog box appears.

4. Type the **Command Line** to start the command line application or open the file.

NOTE: *To view available files, select the* ***Browse*** *button.*

5. Enter **D**ate and **T**ime .... `Alt`+`D`, *date*
   to run program .... `Alt`+`T`, *time*

Application starts or file opens.

6. Change **A**M/**P**M .... `Alt`+`A` or `Alt`+`P`
   setting, if desired.

continued...

Add KickOff Event (continued)

7. Enter interval **Day**(s)/time .... **Alt**+**Y**, *days*

   to indicate when event................ **Alt**+**M**, *time*
   should repeat.

8. Select **Disable** check box .... **Alt**+**I**
   to disable event if an error occurs.

9. Select **Run Minimized** check box.......... **Alt**+**R**
   to run event minimized.

10. Click ⌹ **OK** ⌹ .... **Enter**

11. Click ⌹ **Close** ⌹ .... **Esc**

Edit KickOff Event

1. Exit WordPerfect for Windows 6.1.

   —FROM WORDPERFECT GROUP—

2. Click KickOff

3. Select event to edit.

4. Click ⌹ **E**dit... ⌹ .... **Alt**+**E**

5. Make desired changes.

   *(See **Add KickOff Event**, above, for information on fields
   and **B**rowse button.)*

6. Click ⌹ **OK** ⌹ .... **Enter**

7. Click ⌹ **Close** ⌹ .... **Esc**

Delete KickOff Event(s)

1. Exit WordPerfect for Windows 6.1.

    —FROM WORDPERFECT GROUP—

2. Click KickOff

3. Select event(s) to delete.

4. Click **Remove** .... `Alt`+`R`

5. Click **Yes** .... `Y`
    in **Remove Event** dialog box.

    OR

    Click **No** .... `N`

6. Click **OK** .... `Enter`

7. Click **Close** .... `Esc`

LABELS

*When you create labels in WordPerfect, you have logical pages
and physical pages. Each label is a logical page. Each page
of labels is a physical page. So, for example, you may have
thirty labels (logical pages) on one page of labels (physical
page).*

*Label definitions contain all the predefined information you
need to start creating labels: selected printer model, label type,
and so forth. Groups of label definitions are stored together in
label files.*

View Labels

You can type labels in any view. In Draft mode, however, labels are separated with a dotted line and do not appear the way they will print. To see how labels will print, use Page mode with Zoom (Full Page or Page Width options) or Two Page mode. (See VIEW MODES, page 262, and ZOOM, page 277, for more information.)

Select Label Definition

1. Place cursor on page where labels are to begin.

2. Select **Format** menu .... `Alt` + `R`

3. Select **Labels** .... `B`

4. Choose label type to display.

5. Select desired **Labels** .... `Alt` + `L`, `↑` `↓`
   definition.

6. Click `Select` .... `Enter`

Type Text in Labels

- End text on current label .... `Ctrl` + `Enter`
  and move to next label

- End line of text within label .... `Enter`

- Move to next label .... `Alt` + `Page Up`

- Move to previous label .... `Alt` + `Page Up`

Create/Edit Label Definition

1. Place cursor where label definition is to begin.

2. Select **Format** menu .... **Alt**+**R**

3. Select **Labels** .... **B**

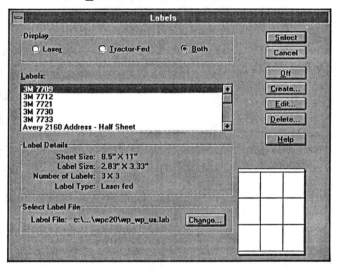

To create new definition:

a. Select definition .... **↑** **↓**

continued...

Create/Edit Label Definition (continued)

b. Click [**Create**] .... **Alt**+**C**

c. Type label description .... *description*

4. Click [**Change...**] .... **Alt**+**A**
   to select different paper size.

   To create new sheet definition:

   a. Click [**Create...**] .... **Alt**+**C**

   b. Indicate paper name, size and location, as well as paper and text orientation.

   c. Click [**OK**] twice...... **Enter**, **Enter**

   OR

   a. Select **Sheet Definition** ... **Alt**+**S**, **↑**/**↓**

   b. Click [**OK**] .... **Enter**

5. Select display option to arrange labels on page.

6. Click [**OK**] .... **Enter**

continued

Create/Edit Label Definition (continued)

To use definition now:

a. Select definition .... `Alt`+`L`, `↑` `↓`

b. Click `Select` .... `Alt`+`S`

Delete Label Definition

1. Select **Format** menu .... `Alt`+`R`

2. Select **Labels** .... `B`

3. Select label type to display.

4. Select **Labels** definition .... `Alt`+`L`, `↑` `↓`

5. Click `Delete...` .... `Alt`+`D`

6. Click `Yes` .... `Enter`

Select Label File

> *NOTE: Changing the label file brings in a new set of label definitions.*

1. Select **Format** menu .... `Alt`+`R`

2. Select **Labels** .... `B`

3. Click `Change...` .... `Alt`+`A`

4. Select desired **Filename** .... `Alt`+`F`, `↑` `↓`

5. Click `Select` .... `Alt`+`S`

continued...

Select Label File (continued)

To select label definition:

a. Select **L**abel definition.... `Alt`+`L`, `↑` `↓`

b. Click `Select` .... `Alt`+`S`

Create/Edit Label File

1. Select **Fo**r**mat** menu .... `Alt`+`R`

2. Select **La**b**els** .... `B`

3. Click `Change...` .... `Alt`+`A`

4. Click `Create...` .... `Alt`+`C`

   OR

   a. Select label **F**ilename...... `Alt`+`F`, `↑` `↓`
      to edit.

   b. Click `Edit...` .... `Alt`+`E`

5. Type **F**ilename .... *filename*

6. Type **D**escription .... `Alt`+`D`, *description*

7. Click `OK` .... `Enter`

8. Click `Select` .... `Alt`+`S`

   To return to document without selecting definition:

   Click `Cancel` .... `Esc`

Delete Label File

1. Select **Fo_r_mat** menu .... `Alt`+`R`

2. Select **La_b_els** .... `B`

3. Click `Ch_a_nge...` .... `Alt`+`A`

4. Select desired .... `Alt`+`F`, `↑` `↓`
   label **_F_ilename**.

   NOTE: You cannot delete an active file.

5. Click `_D_elete...` .... `Alt`+`D`

6. Click `Yes` .... `Enter`

   OR

   Click `_N_o` .... `N`
   to cancel deletion.

7. Click `Cancel` twice .... `Esc`, `Esc`
   to return to document without selecting definition.

Turn Labels Off

1. Select **Fo_r_mat** menu .... `Alt`+`R`

2. Select **La_b_els** .... `B`

3. Click `_O_ff` .... `Alt`+`O`

   *NOTE: When you turn labels off before the end of
   a page, WordPerfect completes the rest of
   the page with blank labels.*

128

Print Specific Labels

1. Click 🖳 .... `Ctrl`+`P`

2. Select **Multiple Pages** .... `M`

3. Click ⬛ **Print...** .... `Enter`

4. Enter page numbers ....*numbers* of labels to print.

5. Click ⬛ **Print** .... `Enter`

(See PRINT, page 171, for more information.)

LANGUAGE

Specifies which language codes to use for dictionary, thesaurus and hyphenation files. Also allows you to specify how words in dates are spelled and what order is used for sorting.

1. Place cursor where new language information should be used, or select desired text.

2. Select **Tools** menus .... `Alt`+`T`

3. Select **Language** .... `L`

4. Select desired language .... `Alt`+`C`, `↓` `↑` from **Current Language** list.

5. Select **Disable Writing Tools (in** .... `Alt`+`D` **this portion of the text)** check box.

6. Click ⬛ **OK** .... `Enter`

LEADING

1. Place insertion point where change is to begin, or select desired text.

2. Select **Fo_r_mat** menu .... |Alt|+|R|

3. Select **_T_ypesetting** .... |T|

4. Select **_W_ord/Letter Spacing** .... |W|

5. Select **Adjust _L_eading** .... |L|

6. Type distance .... |Tab|, *number* in **Be_t_ween Lines** box.

   NOTE: A negative number decreases the space between lines; a positive number increases it.

7. Click [___OK___] .... |Enter|

LINE DRAW

(See GRAPHICS, page 76, and WORDPERFECT DRAW, page 273.)

LINE HEIGHT

1. Place insertion point where change is to begin, or select desired text.

2. Select **Fo_r_mat** menu .... |Alt|+|R|

3. Select **_L_ine** .... |L|

4. Select **_H_eight** .... |H|

continued...

LINE HEIGHT (continued)

To let WordPerfect choose automatic line height setting:

Select **Auto** .... **A**

To choose fixed setting:

a. Select **Fixed** .... **F**

b. Type new height .... **Tab**, *number*

5. Click **OK** .... **Enter**

LINE NUMBERING

Number Lines

1. Place insertion point where numbering is to begin.

    NOTE: Numbering begins on first line of paragraph containing insertion point.

2. Select **Format** menu .... **Alt**+**R**

3. Select **Line**... **L**

4. Select **Numbering**.................................... **N**

5. Select **Turn Line Numbering On** check box..... **O**

6. Select options, as desired.

7. Click **OK** .... **Enter**

    NOTE: To turn line numbers off, repeat steps above, placing insertion point where numbering is to end.

Edit Line Numbers

1. Place insertion point where numbering changes are to begin.

   NOTE: The changes you make begin on the first line of the paragraph containing the insertion point.

2. Select **Fo_r_mat** menu .... `Alt`+`R`

3. Select **L_ine** .... `L`

4. Select **N_umbering** .... `N`

5. Choose desired options.

6. Click `OK` .... `Enter`

LINE SPACING

(See LEADING, page 129, and LINE HEIGHT, page 129, for additional information.)

1. Place insertion point where you would like change to begin, or select desired text.

2. Click `1.0 ▼` on power bar.

3. Select **1.0**, **1.5** or **2.0** for single, space and a half or double spacing.

   OR

   a.   Select **Other**.

   b.   Enter desired line spacing. .... *number*

4. Click `OK` .... `Enter`

LIST

Creates a list of illustrations, tables, etc. To create a list, you must complete the following three steps:

1. *Mark items to include in the list.*
2. *Define the list style and location.*
3. *Generate the list.*

Mark List Text

To display List feature bar:

Click 🗒................................ **Alt**+**T**, **I**
on Generate Toolbar.

The List feature bar appears.

| ❓ List: | ▼ | Mark | Define... | Close | Generate... |

1. Type/select **List** name...... **Shift**+**Alt**+**L**, *name*

2. Select word(s) to include in list.

3. Click Mark .... **Shift**+**Alt**+**M**

4. Repeat steps 2–3 for every entry in list.

Define List

1. Place insertion point where list is to appear.

2. Type title (e.g., Illustrations)............................*title*

3. Press **Enter**...**Enter**
for spacing, as desired.

—WITH LIST FEATURE BAR ACTIVE—

4. Click Define... .... **Shift**+**Alt**+**D**

continued.

To define list for which you have already marked entries:

a. Select list............................ ↑ ↓ , Enter
   to define.

b. Click [Edit...] .... Alt + E

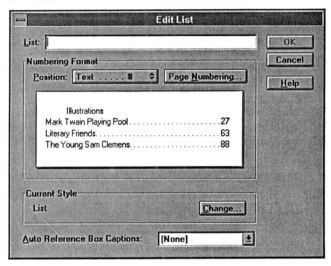

To define new list:

a. Click [Create...] .... Alt + A

b. Type list name ....*list name*

*NOTE: If you are creating a list from existing captions of graphics boxes, select the type of caption from the **Auto Reference Box Captions** drop–down list.*

To retrieve definition from another document:

a. Click [Retrieve...] .... Alt + R

continued...

Define List (continued)

    b.   Type document name.............. *document name* containing definition.

    c.   Click **Insert** .... `Enter`

    d.   Select desired definition....... `↑` `↓`, `Enter`

    e.   Click **OK** .... `Enter`

To choose page numbering position:

    a.   Click **Position...** .... `Alt`+`P`

    b.   Choose desired options.

To change page numbering format:

    a.   Click **Page Numbering...** .... `Alt`+`N`

    b.   Select **Document Page Number** ...... `Alt`+`D` **Format** to return to document page number format.

NOTE: *To create a user defined page number format, see **PAGE NUMBERING**, page 160.*

    c.   Click **OK** .... `Enter`

5.   Click **OK** .... `Enter`

To insert definition into your document:

    a.   Select list.............................. `↑` `↓`, `Enter`

    b.   Click **Insert ▼** .... `Alt`+`I`

<<List will generate here>> appears under your title.

Generate List

—WITH GENERATE TOOLBAR/LIST FEATURE BAR ACTIVE—

1. Click 🔄 .... Shift + Alt + G

*The **Generate** dialog box appears.*

2. Click **Options...** .... O
   if desired.

3. Select one of the following check box options:

   a. Select **Save Subdocuments** .... S
      if generating list for master document
      and want to save generated subdocuments.

   b. Click **OK** .... Enter

   OR

   a. Select **Build Hypertext Links** .... B
      if generating list for document containing
      hypertext links and want links created.

   b. Click **OK** .... Enter

4. Click **OK** .... Enter

List appears.

(See GENERATE, page 72, for additional information.)

LOCATION OF FILES

*(See **PREFERENCES**, page 170.)*

MACROS

Record Macro

CAUTION: Do not use a mouse to record a macro.

1. Click ⌨ on Macro Tools Toolbar.

   NOTES: To access Macro Tools Toolbar, select
   ***Edit, Preferences, Toolbar** and **Select**
   button.

   *To store in a location other than the
   default, see **Change Location**, below.*

2. Type macro filename ....*filename.wcm*

   *NOTE: If you select **Location** and indicate **Current**
   ***Document** or **New Document**, you will not
   be asked for a filename.*

3. Click [**Record**] ....**Alt**+**R**

Macro feature bar appears.

| ? | ■ | ⟳ | ▶ | ❚❚ | Dialog Editor... | Commands... | Save & Compile | Codes... | Options ▼ |

4. Use WordPerfect to record desired commands.

   To stop recording:

   Press **Ctrl+F10**......................................**Ctrl**+**F10**

Change Location

Allows you to specify a location to record to before recording.

   *NOTE: These keystrokes also work during Play
   and Edit procedures.*

   —FROM RECORD MACRO DIALOG BOX—

1. Select **Location**....................................**Alt**+**L**

Change Location (continued)

continued

To indicate location:
Choose one of the following options:

- **C**urrent Template........................ Alt + C
- **F**ile on Disk............................... Alt + F
- Cu**r**rent Document....................... Alt + R
- **N**ew Document............................ Alt + N

NOTE: *If you choose **Current Document** or **New***
Document in this step, the macro must be
saved to the current template, default
template, or a disk file before it is played.

To use setting as default:

Select **U**se as Default check box .... Alt + U

2. Click [OK] .... Enter

Play Back Macro

NOTE: *The last macro you record or play is*
*displayed on the **Macro** menu. To play a*
macro from the menu, select the macro.

1. Place insertion point where macro is to begin.

2. Click 🖼 .... Alt + T, M, P
on Macro Tools Toolbar.

3. Type macro filename .... *macro filename*
or select desired one from **File**n**ame** list.

4. Click [Play] .... Alt + P

Edit Macro

> *NOTE:* *You can also edit a macro that has been saved to a file on disk by retrieving it into a document window.*

1. Click [image] .... **Alt**+**T**, **M**, **E**
   on Macro Tools Toolbar.

2. Type name of macro...................................... *name*
   to edit.

3. Click [**E**dit] .... **E**

4. Type new commands...................... *new commands*
   and/or edit existing commands
   *(see also **Use Command Inserter**, below).*

5. Press **Ctrl+F4**.. **Ctrl**+**F4**
   when finished editing macro.

Use Command Inserter

> *NOTE:* *To access Macro Tools Toolbar, select **Edit**, **Preferences**, **Toolbar** and click **Select** button.*

1. Click [Co**m**mands...] .... **Shift**+**Alt**+**M**

The WordPerfect Command Inserter dialog box appears.

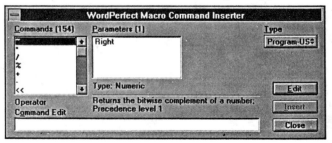

continued

Use Command Inserter (continued)

2. Select command .... `Alt`+`T`, `F4`, `↑``↓`
   Type from pop-up list.

3. Select desired **Commands** ..... `Alt`+`C`, `↑``↓`
   from scroll down list.

If command you chose in step 3 has parameters:

Select from **Parameters** list ... `Alt`+`P`, `↑``↓`

If command you chose in step 3 has members:

Select from **Members** list....... `Alt`+`M`, `↑``↓`

If you need additional parameters/values:

The insertion point is positioned in the macro.

Enter parameters.... `Alt`+`O`, *parameters/values*
in **Command Edit** box.

4. Click `Insert` .... `Alt`+`I`

5. Click `Close` .... `Esc`
   to return to your document.

Compile Macro

NOTE: *If an error message appears during*
compiling, you can either fix the error or
continue. A macro will not play until all
errors are corrected, however.

140

MAKE IT FIT EXPERT

Lets you automatically adjust document to fit specified number of pages.

1. Open or create document.

2. Click 🔍 .... **Ctrl**+**R**, **I**
   on default Toolbar.

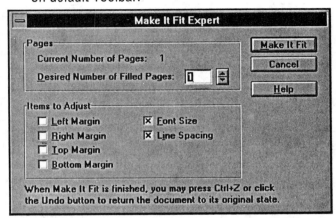

3. Enter **Desired Number of Filled Pages** ..... *number*

4. Select **Items to Adjust** automatically.

5. Click **Make It Fit** .... **Alt**+**M**

MARGINS

Change Margins/Ruler

> *NOTE:* If ruler bar is not active, press
> **Shift+Alt+F3**.

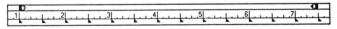

1. Place insertion point in paragraph where you wish to change left and/or right margin(s), or select desired text.

continued

2. Drag margin marker ▆ to new position.

The status bar displays the position of the marker as it is moved (see below).

> Left margin: 1.1 "

Change Margins/Dialog Box

1. Place insertion point in paragraph or page for which you wish to change left and/or right margin(s), or select desired paragraph.

2. Select **Format** menu .... `Alt`+`R`

3. Select **Margins**.. `M`

4. Select text box of margin to change.

5. Enter new margin setting ....*number*

   NOTE: Zero (0) is the edge of the page.

6. Repeat steps 4–5 to make another margin change from the current insertion point position.

7. Click `OK` .... `Enter`

   NOTE: When typing a measurement, you can type a fraction. WordPerfect will convert your fraction to a decimal.

MASTER DOCUMENT

Divides large documents into manageable subdocuments.

Master Document vs. Subdocuments

A master document is like any other document, but it contains codes to link it to subdocuments.

continued...

142

Master Documents vs. Subdocuments (continued)

In Draft mode, the link looks like a shaded comment bar. In Page and Two Page mode, the link appears as an icon. To see complete information on a link, click the Comment feature bar or icon.

> *NOTE: Comment bars and icons do not print.*

Display/Print Master Document

Before you can display and/or print a master document, you must expand it. This process retrieves some or all of the subdocuments (see Expand Master Document, page 143).

The opposite of expand is condense (see Condense Master Document, page 143). During the Condense procedure you can save changes made to the subdocuments.

Format Master Document/Subdocuments

WordPerfect treats formatting commands in an expanded master document just as they are in a regular document; in other words, new commands replace old commands.

> *NOTE: For commands in a subdocument to take effect, the master document must be expanded.*

Insert Subdocuments in Master Document

1. Open file to use as master document, or create a new one.

2. Place insertion point where you want to place subdocument link.

3. Select **File** menu .... `Alt`+`F`

4. Select **Master Document** .... `D`

continued.

Insert Subdocuments in Master Document (cont)

5. Select **Su̲bdocument**................................. 🅂

6. Type filename...*filename*
   or select desired one from **File̲name** list.

7. Click ▭ **Include** ▭ .... 🄰🄻🅃+🄸

8. Repeat steps 2–7 for each subdocument link.

Expand Master Document

1. Select **F̲ile** menu .... 🄰🄻🅃+🄵

2. Select **Master D̲ocument** ....🄳

3. Select **E̲xpand Master** ....🄴

4. Select desired **Su̲bdocuments** to expand.

   NOTE: If a subdocument contains a password,
   you will be prompted to enter the
   password during the Expand procedure.
   *Enter the password and press the **Cancel***
   button to skip the file.

   OR

   Click ▭ **M̲ark** ▾ ▭ .... 🄰🄻🅃+🄼, 🄵🄴, ⬆⬇
   and select desired option from pop–up list.

5. Click ▭ **OK** ▭ ....🄴🄽🅃🄴🅁

Condense Master Document

1. Select **F̲ile** menu .... 🄰🄻🅃+🄵

2. Select **Master D̲ocument** ....🄳

continued...

Condense Master Document (continued)

3. Select **Condense Master** ....

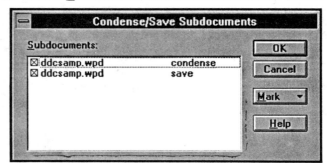

4. Select desired **Subdocuments** to condense/save.
    OR
    Click Mark ▼ ....
    and select desired option from pop–up list.

5. Click OK .... Enter

Edit/Save Master Document

Allows you to edit subdocument text in an expanded master document. During Condense procedure (see above), you can save the changes you make.

> *NOTE: If you save a master document and do not condense, changes will not be made in the subdocument(s).*

Generate Items in Master Document

To create generated items (e.g., Index, Table of Contents, etc.), mark text in subdocuments. Place definitions in subdocuments or master document, as desired.

> *NOTE: You can generate items from a condensed master document. WordPerfect expands the master document, generates the items and condenses the master document.*

MERGE

Form vs. Data Files

*Merge procedures combine a **form file** with a series of records from a **data file**. The merge procedure is controlled by the form file.*

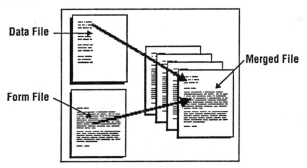

Data File

Form File

Merged File

Data Files

*You can create two different types of data files—text or table. In any **data file**, information is divided into records and fields. For example, one record might contain a name, title and address for one person. Therefore, **Name**, **Title** and **Address** are the three fields in the record.*

*In a **data text file**, a special ENDFIELD command and a hard return ends each field. A special ENDRECORD command and hard page break ends each record.*

*In a **data table file**, the first row contains field names. Then, each cell is a field and each row is a record.*

146

Create Data File

Press **Shift+F9** .... <kbd>Shift</kbd>+<kbd>F9</kbd>

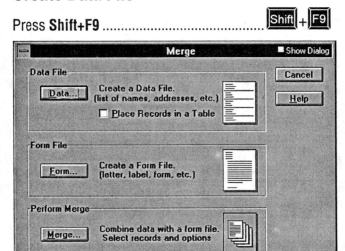

Merge dialog box (see above) and feature bar appear.

| ? | End Field | End Record | Merge Codes... | Quick Entry... | Merge... | Go to Form | Options ▼ |

To create data table file:

a. Select **Place Records** .... <kbd>P</kbd>
   in a Table check box.

b. Click <kbd>Data...</kbd> .... <kbd>D</kbd>

To create data text file:

Click <kbd>Data...</kbd> .... <kbd>D</kbd>

*NOTE: If a document is currently displayed, a
          prompt appears asking if you want to use
          the current document; click **Alt+U** or **Alt+N**
          and **Enter**, as desired.*

continued.

Create Data File (continued)

Create Data File

Name a Field:

Field Name List:

TITLE
ADDRESS

OK
Cancel
Add
Replace
Delete
Move Up
Move Down
Help

Divide your information into categories, and think of a word that describes each category. This is a field name. Add each field name one at a time.

To name each field:

a. Type field name .... *field name*
   in **Name a Field** text box.

b. Click ⎡ **Add** ⎤ .... Enter

c. Repeat steps a-b for each field to name.

d. Click ⎡ **OK** ⎤ .... Enter

2. Enter information for first record ....*first record*

   NOTE: To move to next field, click **Next Field**
   button. To add a line to a field, press
   Ctrl+Enter.

3. Click ⎡ **New Record** ⎤ .... Enter

continued...

Create Data File (continued)

4. Repeat steps above for each record to complete entering records.

5. Click [**Close**] .... [Esc]

   To save file:

   a. Click [**Yes**] .... [Enter]

   b. Type filename..................................... *filename*

   c. Click [**OK**] .... [Enter]

      OR

      Click [**No**] .... [N]

      not to save file.

Edit Data File

—WITH MERGE FEATURE BAR ACTIVE—

1. Create or retrieve data file.

2. Click `Quick Entry...` .... **Shift**+**Alt**+**Q**

   To delete record:

   a. Display record.

   b. Click **Delete Record** .... **Alt**+**D**

   *CAUTION: Deletion is not confirmed, but may be restored. (See **UNDO**, page 260.)*

   To create new record:

   Click **New Record** .... **Alt**+**R**

3. Click **Close** .... **Esc**

4. Click **Yes** .... **Enter**
   to save changes.

5. Type filename .... *filename*

6. Click **OK** .... **Enter**

Sort Data Files

1. Create or retrieve a data file.

2. Click `Options ▼` .. .. **Shift**+**Alt**+**O**

   *(See **SORT**, page 194, for more information.)*

3. Select **Sort** .... **S**

150

Print Data Text Files

1. Create or retrieve a data file.

2. Click `Options ▼` .... `Shift`+`Alt`+`O`

3. Select **Print**.. `P`

4. Click `OK` .... `Enter`

Create Form File

—WITH MERGE FEATURE BAR ACTIVE—

1. Click `Form...` .... `F`

   NOTE: *If a document is currently displayed, a*
   prompt appears asking if you want to use
   the current document or a new one; press
   ***U** or **N** and **Enter**, as desired.*

   ### To associate a data file with this form file:
   a. Type data filename .... *data filename*

   b. Click `OK` .... `Enter`

   ### If data file does not exist for this form file:
   a. Select **None**.................................... `Alt`+`N`

   b. Click `OK` .... `Enter`

2. Format and type document as usual.

   ### To indicate field:
   a. Select **Insert Field**................ `Shift`+`Alt`+`F`

   b. Enter field name/number.... *field name/number*

   c. Click `Insert` .... `Alt`+`I`

continued

Create Form File (continued)

3. Add required text or spacing between fields.

4. Repeat steps 2-3 until form file is complete.

5. Click **Close** .... **Esc**
   from **Insert Field Name** window.

To save file:

Complete Save procedure *(see **SAVE**, page 188)*.

OR

Perform Merge procedure *(see **Perform Merge**, below)*.

Insert Merge Codes

Inserts a merge code at any time when the Merge feature bar is displayed.

1. Place insertion point where you wish to insert code.

2. Click **Merge Codes...** .... **Shift**+**Alt**+**C**

3. Highlight desired code........................... **↑ ↓**

4. Enter additional parameters .... *parameters* if necessary.

5. Click **Insert** .... **Alt**+**I**

6. Click **Close** .... **Esc**

Perform Merge

—WITH MERGE FEATURE BAR ACTIVE—

NOTE: *If Merge feature bar is displayed, press **Shift+Alt+M** to get to Merge window.*

continued...

Perform Merge (continued)

1. Click ⎣ **Merge...** ⎦ .... **M**

2. Select desired ...... **Alt**+**F**, **F4**, **S**, *filename*
   Form File from pop-up list.

3. Select desired ...... **Alt**+**D**, **F4**, **S**, *filename*
   Data File from pop-up list.

   OR

   Select **<None>** if performing keyboard merge.

4. Select desired .... **Alt**+**U**, **F4**, **S**, *path/name*
   Output File from pop-up list.

5. Choose desired **Perform Merge Options** buttons.

6. Click ⎣ **Reset** ⎦ .... **Alt**+**R**
   to clear all options.

7. Click ⎣ **OK** ⎦ .... **Enter**

Select Records to Merge

*Records may be selected according to predetermined
conditions or by marking records.*

continued

Select Records to Merge (continued)

1. Complete steps 1–5, **Perform** .... `Alt`+`S`
   Merge, above (choose **Select Records**).

2. Select **Mark Records** button .... `Alt`+`A`

   To indicate records to display:

   a. Enter first number .... `Alt`+`D`, *number*
      in **Display Records From** box.

   b. Enter last number in **To** box ..... `Tab`, *number*

   To indicate first field to display for each record:
   Select field .... `Alt`+`F`, `F4`, `↑``↓`, `Enter`
   from **First Field to Display** list.

   *NOTE: Record display starts from specified field
   position and continues through end of
   each record.*

3. Select **Update Record List** .... `Alt`+`U`
   to display selected records.

4. Select records .... `Alt`+`L`, `↑``↓`, `Enter`
   to merge in **Records List**.

   OR

   Select **Mark all Records** .... `Alt`+`M`

   OR

   Select **Unmark all Records** .... `Alt`+`U`

5. Click [OK] twice .... `Enter`, `Enter`
   to perform merge.

154

Create Keyboard Merge

1. Create or retrieve form file.

   —WITH MERGE FEATURE BAR ACTIVE—

2. Select **K**eyboard .... `Shift`+`Alt`+`K`

3. Type desired prompt................................... *prompt*

4. Click `OK` .... `Enter`

Use Keyboard Merge

Complete steps 1–4 **Perform Merge**, page 151.

Merge Message prompt appears.

   a. Enter requested information..................... *data*

   b. Select **C**ontinue button .... `Alt`+`C`

   To ignore next record before leaving current one:

   Select S**k**ip Record button..................... `Alt`+`K`

   To quit Merge procedure at end and ignore all merge commands from current position to end:

   Select **Q**uit button................................. `Alt`+`Q`

   To stop merge procedure at current position:

   Select **S**top button .... `Alt`+`S`

Convert Other WordPerfect Versions

If you use data or form files created with previous versions of WordPerfect, the files are automatically converted to WordPerfect 6.1 during the Merge process.

NEW DOCUMENT WINDOW

Click ⬜ .... **Alt**+**F**, **N**

OPEN DOCUMENT WINDOW

1. Click 📂 .... **Alt**+**F**, **O**
2. Type or select desired filename .... *filename*
3. Click ⬛ OK .... **Enter**

OTHER CODES

1. Place insertion point where code is to appear.
2. Select **Format** menu .... **Alt**+**R**
3. Select **Line** .... **L**
4. Select **Other Codes** .... **O**
5. Choose desired **Other Codes** options.
6. Click ⬛ Insert .... **Enter**

OUTLINE

Create Outline

1. Place insertion point where outline is to begin.

   To display Outline feature bar:
   Click ⬛ .... **Alt**+**T**, **O**
   on Legal Toolbar.

⬛⬛⬛⬛⬛⬛⬛ ⬛⬛ Show Outline Levels ▾ Hide Body Text Options ▾ Paragraph ⬍ Close

continued...

Create Outline (continued)

NOTE: *The default outline style is paragraph. To change to a different outline style, select from the drop–down list beside the outline style text box on the feature bar.*

2. Type outline text ....*text*

To insert next outline number for current level:

Press **Enter**... Enter

If there is no text on current line, WordPerfect adds a blank line.

To change to next outline level:
a. Place insertion point immediately to right or left of existing outline number.

b. Press ⟫⟶ .... Tab
until desired number or outline level appears.

To change to previous outline level:
a. Place insertion point immediately to right or left of outline number to change.

b. Press ⟵⟪ .... Shift + Tab
until desired number for outline level appears.

To delete outline number:
a. Place insertion point immediately to right of outline number to delete.

b. Press **Backspace**........................... Backspace

Turn Outline Off

—WITH OUTLINE FEATURE BAR ACTIVE—

1. Place insertion point where outline is to end.

2. Click Options ▼ .... Shift + Alt + O

continued

3. Select **End Outline**.......................................🅔

4. Click [__Close__] ....**Shift**+**Alt**+**C**

Renumber Outline

—WITH OUTLINE FEATURE BAR ACTIVE—

1. Place insertion point where renumbering is to begin.

3. Click [Options ▼] ....**Shift**+**Alt**+**O**

4. Select **Set Number** ....🅢

5. Enter number ....*start number* to start with in **Paragraph Number** text box.

6. Click [__OK__] ....**Enter**

Create/Edit Outline Definition

—WITH OUTLINE FEATURE BAR ACTIVE—

1. Click [Options ▼] ....**Shift**+**Alt**+**O**

2. Select **Define Outline**...................................🅓

continued..

Create/Edit Outline Definition (continued)

3. Select definition .... ⬇️ ⬆️
   to edit.

4. Click [E̲dit...] .... Alt + E
   If creating definition:

   a. Type name.................................... *outline name*

   b. Type description............................. *description*

5. Make desired changes, selections, etc....... ⬆️ ⬇️

6. Click [OK] .... Enter

OVERSTRIKE CHARACTERS

Create Overstrike Character

1. Place insertion point where overstrike character is
   to appear, or select desired text.

2. Select **Fo̲rmat** menu .... Alt + R

3. Select **T̲ypesetting** .... T

4. Select **O̲verstrike** .... O

5. Type two **Cha̲racters** .... *characters*
   to overstrike two characters.

   *NOTE: Order is not important. Also, no spaces
   should appear between the characters.*

6. Click [OK] .... Enter

Edit Overstrike Character

—WITH REVEAL CODES WINDOW ACTIVE—

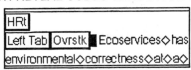

1. Double–click `Ovrstk`

   To see next overstrike character:

   Click `Next` .... `Alt`+`N`

   To see previous overstrike character in document:

   Click `Prev` .... `Alt`+`R`

2. Edit characters, as desired.

   NOTE: To restore original contents, click Redo button.

3. Click `Close` .... `Esc`

PAGE BREAK

Insert Hard Page Break

1. Place insertion point where new page is to begin.

2. Press **Ctrl+Enter** (Page Break) .... `Ctrl`+`Enter`

A double horizontal line appears to indicate page break.

Delete Page Break

1. Place insertion point directly beneath page break.

2. Press **Backspace** .... `Backspace`

160

PAGE BORDERS

(See BORDERS, page 12.)

PAGE NUMBERING

Number Pages

1. Place insertion point where numbering is to begin.

2. Click #1 .... Alt + R , P , N
   on Page Toolbar.

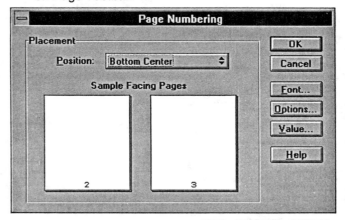

3. Select location .... F4 , ↓ ↑ , Enter
   in **Position** pop-up list.

Page number placement appears in Sample Facing Pages portion of the dialog box.

4. Click OK .... Enter

Include Text with Page Numbers

1. Place cursor where you wish to edit page numbers.

continued.

Include Text with Page Numbers (continued)

2. Click 🔲 .... `Alt`+`R`, `P`, `N`
   on Page Toolbar.

3. Click **Options...** .... `Alt`+`O`

4. Type text.. *text*
   in **Format and Accompanying Text** text box.

5. Click **OK** twice .... `Enter`, `Enter`

Include Chapter, Volume, Secondary Page Numbers

1. Place insertion point where changes are to begin.

2. Click 🔲 .... `Alt`+`R`, `P`, `N`
   on Page Toolbar.

3. Click **Options...** .... `Alt`+`O`

Page Numbering Options		
Number Type		OK
Format and Accompanying Text:		Cancel
[ ] Insert ▾		Help
Page: Numbers ⬍		
Secondary: Numbers ⬍		
Chapter: Numbers ⬍		
Volume: Numbers ⬍		
Sample Facing Pages		
☐ **Insert Format and Accompanying Text at Insertion Point**		

continued...

Include Chapter, Vol., Secondary Pg. Numbers (cont)

4. Click ⌊Insert ▼⌋ .... [Alt]+[I], [F4]

5. Select desired number type .... [↑] [↓], [Enter]

6. Click ⌊ OK ⌋ twice .... [Enter], [Enter]

Increase/Decrease Numbers

1. Place insertion point where changes are to begin.

2. Click [#1] .... [Alt]+[R], [P], [N]
   on Page Toolbar.

3. Click ⌊Value...⌋ .... [Alt]+[V]

Numbering Value

Page Settings
New Page Number: 1
Increase/Decrease Existing Page Number: 0
☐ Insert and Display at Insertion Point

Secondary Settings
New Secondary Number: 1
Increase/Decrease Existing Secondary Number: 0
☐ Insert and Display at Insertion Point

Chapter Settings
New Chapter Number: 1
Increase/Decrease Existing Chapter Number: 0
☐ Insert and Display at Insertion Point

Volume Settings
New Volume Number: 1
Increase/Decrease Existing Volume Number: 0
☐ Insert and Display at Insertion Point

OK   Cancel   Help

4. Enter interval .... *interval*
   by which you would like to increase/
   decrease selected number type.

5. Click ⌊ OK ⌋ twice .... [Enter], [Enter]

Set New Numbers

1. Place insertion point where changes are to begin.

2. Click `[#1]` .... `Alt`+`R`, `P`, `N`
   on Page Toolbar.

3. Click `Value...` .... `Alt`+`V`

4. Enter new number type .... *new number type*

5. Click `OK` twice .... `Enter`, `Enter`

Change Font/Appearance of Numbers

1. Place insertion point where changes are to begin.

2. Click `[#1]` .... `Alt`+`R`, `P`, `N`
   on Page Toolbar.

3. Click `Font...` .... `Alt`+`F`

4. Select desired option(s).

5. Click `OK` twice .... `Enter`, `Enter`

Change Number Type

1. Place insertion point where changes are to begin.

2. Click `[#1]` .... `Alt`+`R`, `P`, `N`
   on Page Toolbar.

3. Click `Options...` .... `Shift`+`Alt`+`O`

4. Select new .... `Alt`+*letter*, `F4`, `↓`, `↑`, `Enter`
   type from **Page**, **Se**condary, **Chapter**,
   or **Volume** list.

5. Click `OK` twice .... `Enter`, `Enter`

Force Odd/Even/New Page

Ensures a page always starts a specified way. This feature can, for example, make sure a chapter always begins on an odd-numbered page.

1. Place insertion point on desired page.

2. Click 🔳 .... `Alt`+`R`, `P`, `F`
   on Page Toolbar.

3. Select desired **Force** option.

4. Click `OK` .... `Enter`

PAGE VIEW

(See VIEW MODES, page 262.)

PAPER SIZE

Select Paper Definition

1. Place insertion point where changes are to begin.

2. Click 🔳 .... `Alt`+`R`, `P`, `S`
   on Page Toolbar.

3. Highlight desired **Paper Definition** .... `↑` `↓`

   To use existing paper definition as guide:

   a. Highlight similar definition .... `↑` `↓`

   b. Click `Create...` .... `Alt`+`R`

   c. Type unique **Paper Name** .... *definition name*

   d. Select **Paper Type** .... `Alt`+`T`, `F4`, `↑` `↓`
      from **Type** list.

continued

Select Paper Definition (continued)

e. Select **Paper Size** .... [Alt]+[S], [F4], [↑][↓]
   from **Size** list.

f. Select **Paper** .... [Alt]+[L], [F4], [↑][↓]
   Location from **Location** list.

*NOTE: For a WordPerfect printer driver, the
        default setting is upper tray or the
        continuous feed location. For a Windows
        printer driver, the default setting is
        specified in the Windows Print Manager.*

g. Select **Rotated Font** check box .... [Alt]+[F]
   to rotate font.

h. Select **Wide Form** check box .... [Alt]+[W]
   to print wide form.

i. Specify **Top** .... [Alt]+*letter*, [F4], [Tab], *number*
   and **Side** adjustments
   to adjust where text prints.

j. Click [OK   ] .... [Enter]
   to save definition.

4. Click [Select] .... [Enter]

Edit Paper Definition

1. Click [📋] .... [Alt]+[R], [P], [S]
   on Page Toolbar.

2. Highlight desired **Paper Definition** .... [↑][↓]

continued...

166

Edit Paper Definition (continued)

To delete paper definition:

a. Click **Delete...** .... Alt + D

b. Click **Yes** .... Y

c. Click **Close** .... Esc

NOTE: When you delete a definition, WordPerfect cannot use it in a document. If WordPerfect encounters a deleted definition during formatting or printing, it looks for a similar definition. If one is not found, it uses the [ALL OTHERS] definition. This is true only if you are using a WordPerfect printer driver.

3. Click **Edit...** .... Alt + E

4. Make necessary edit(s).

5. Click **OK** twice .... Enter, Enter

6. Click **Close** .... Esc

PARAGRAPH BORDERS

(See BORDERS, page 12.)

(See BORDERS, page 12.)

PARAGRAPH FORMAT

Change Format Options

1. Place insertion point where changes are to begin, or select desired text.

2. Click ▦ .... Alt + R, A, F
   on default Toolbar.

Change Format Options (continued)

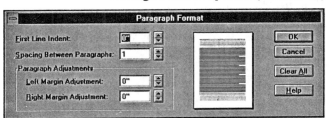

To have first line of paragraph indent specific amount when you press Enter:
Enter desired indent measurement.............*number* in **F**irst Line Indent text box.

To have additional spacing between paragraphs when you press Enter:

a. Select **S**pacing Between Paragraphs...... **Tab**

b. Enter spacing amount.........................*number*

NOTE: *Spacing between paragraphs will be line spacing setting times the number entered in the step b above.*

To adjust margins:

a. Select **L**eft Margin Adjustment .... **Tab**
    OR
    Select **R**ight Margin Adjustment .... **Tab**, **Tab**

b. Enter adjustment measurement...........*number*

3. Click [**OK**] ....**Enter**

NOTE: *To return to previous settings, place insertion point where paragraph settings should be reset and press **Alt+R**, **A**, **F**, **Alt+A** and press **Enter**.*

continued...

PARAGRAPH NUMBERING

(See OUTLINE, page 155.)

PASSWORD

(See SAVE, page 188.)

PASTE

Repositions what was previously copied or cut to the Windows clipboard.

1. Complete Copy or Cut procedure *(see **COPY OR CUT (MOVE) DATA**, page 31).*

2. Click 🖼 .... `Ctrl`+`V`

   NOTE: Copied or cut information remains on the clipboard until it is replaced with another selection.

POWER BAR

Use the mouse to access commonly used features.

| Times New Roman ▼ | 12 pt ▼ | Styles ▼ | Left ▼ | 1.0 ▼ | Tables ▼ | Columns ▼ | 91% ▼ |

Display/Hide Power Bar

   NOTE: To use the power bar, you must use a mouse.

1. Select **V**iew .... `Alt`+`V`

2. Select **P**ower Bar .... `O`

   To hide Power Bar:

   a. Right-click on power bar.

   b. Select **H**ide Power Bar .... `H`

Customize Power Bar

1. Right-click on power bar.

2. Click **Options**..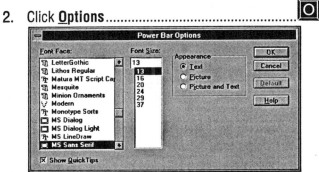

3. Select desired options.

4. Click [**OK**] .... Enter

Edit Power Bar

1. Right-click on power bar.

2. Click **Edit**... E

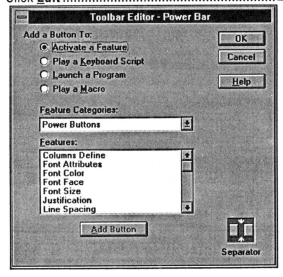

continued...

Edit Power Bar (continued)

3. Select desired options.

4. Click [OK   ] .... Enter

PREFERENCES

Lets you customize WordPerfect since many options are preset. If preset settings work well for you, however, you may never need to set preferences.

1. Select **Edit** menu .... Alt + E

2. Select **Preferences** .... E

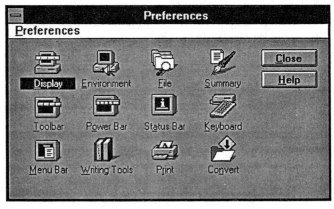

3. Double–click desired .... Alt +*letter,* Enter
   Preferences icon.

4. Make desired changes.

5. Click [OK   ] .... Enter

6. Click [Close   ] .... Alt + C

PRINT

Select Printer Driver

1. Press **Ctrl+P** .... Ctrl + P

2. Click **Select...** .... S

3. Highlight printer .... Tab, F4, ↓, ↑, Enter

   OR

   Select **High** .... Alt + Q, F4, ↓, ↑, Enter
   Medium or **Draft** from **Print Quality** list.

   *NOTE: When using this procedure, be aware that
   the higher the print quality selected, the
   more time and memory printing requires.*

4. Click **Close** .... Esc

Print File

1. Open file to print.

2. Click 🖨 .... Ctrl + P

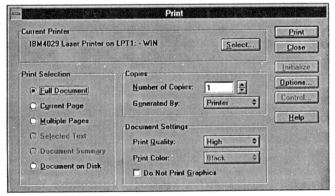

Print File (continued)

3. Choose desired **Print Selection** option(s).

   NOTES: *Selected Text option is available only if text has been selected.*

   Document Summary option is available only if you have created a document summary.

   If desired printer is not the current printer, see Select Printer Driver, above.

   To print multiple copies:

   a. Select **Number of Copies** .... $\boxed{\text{N}}$

   b. Enter desired number.......................... *number* in text box.

   To print only desired pages:

   a. Select **Multiple Pages**.......................... $\boxed{\text{M}}$

   b. Enter desired print range.................... *number*

4. Click $\boxed{\text{Print...}}$ .... $\boxed{\text{P}}$

   NOTE: *To cancel print job, click Print button on Toolbar, click Control button to display the WordPerfect Print Job dialog box and select Cancel Print Job.*

PRINTERS

1. Press **Ctrl+P** .... $\boxed{\text{Ctrl}}$+$\boxed{\text{P}}$
2. Click $\boxed{\text{Select...}}$ .... $\boxed{\text{Alt}}$+$\boxed{\text{A}}$,$\boxed{\text{F4}}$
3. Click $\boxed{\text{Add Printer } \blacktriangledown}$ .... $\boxed{\text{Alt}}$+$\boxed{\text{A}}$,$\boxed{\text{↓}}$

continued

4. Select **WordPerfect** .... P
   to add WordPerfect printer driver.

   OR

   Select **Windows** .... W
   to add Windows printer driver.

   NOTE: *To continue to add a WordPerfect printer*
   driver, follow the steps below. To add a
   *Windows printer driver, click **Add>>***
   button.

5. Select **Printer Files (*.prs)** .... Alt + P
   If desired printer is not listed among Printers:

   a. Select **Additional Printers** .... Alt + D

      OR

      Click ⎡ **Add >>** ⎤ .... Alt + A

   b. Select printer(s) .... ↓ ↑ , Enter
      to add.

   c. Click ⎡ **Install...** ⎤ .... Enter

   If Create Printer dialog box appears:

   a. Confirm or specify filename .... *filename*

   b. Click ⎡ **OK** ⎤ .... Enter

   The printer is now added to the Installed Printers list.

174

Display Printer Information

1. Press **Ctrl+P** .... `Ctrl`+`P`

2. Click `Select` .... `Alt`+`S`

3. Click `Add Printer ▼` .... `Alt`+`A`, `F4`

4. Select **Word_Perfect** .... `P`
   to add WordPerfect printer driver.

   OR

   Select **Windows** .... `W`
   to add Windows printer driver.

   *NOTE: To continue to add a WordPerfect printer
   driver, follow the steps below.*

5. Select **Printer Files (*.prs)** .... `Alt`+`P`

6. Select printer .... `↓` `↑`, `Enter`
   for which you need information.

7. Click `Info...` .... `Alt`+`I`

8. Press **Esc** three times .... `Esc`, `Esc`, `Esc`

Printer Setup

1. Press **Ctrl+P** .... `Ctrl`+`P`

2. Click `Select` .... `Alt`+`S`

3. Select **Specific Printer** .... `Alt`+`E`

continued.

4. Highlight WordPerfect printer ...... ↓ ↑, Enter
   to setup.

5. Select **Setup** .... Alt + E

6. Enter and edit options.

7. Click [OK] .... Enter

   To make new printer current printer:

   a. Highlight desired printer .... ↓ ↑, Enter

   b. Click [Select] .... Alt + S

Insert Printer Commands

1. Place insertion point where you wish to insert print
   command into document.

2. Select **Format** menu .... Alt + R

3. Select **Typesetting** .... T

4. Select **Printer Command** .... P

5. Do one of the following:

   a. Select **Command** .... Alt + C

   b. Type printer command .... *printer command*

   OR

   a. Select **Printer Command Filename** .. Alt + P

   b. Type filename .... *filename*

continued...

176

6. Select **P<u>a</u>use Printer**..............................
   to pause printer when it reaches
   current insertion point.

   > *NOTE:* *When the printer pauses, the you are*
   > *prompted to restart the print job. When*
   > *the print job restarts, it resumes printing*
   > *where it stopped.*

7. Click [**OK**] .... Enter

QUICKCORRECT

*Automatically corrects spelling errors, capitalization mistakes
and other common typing errors. Also expands abbreviations.*

1. Select **<u>T</u>ools**... Alt + T

2. Select **<u>Q</u>uickCorrect**.................................... Q

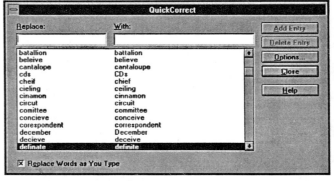

3. Type word to **<u>R</u>eplace** in text box.

   OR

   Type abbreviation to expand.

continued

4. Type correct spelling of word in **With** text box.

   OR

   Type exapanded word(s) of abbreviation.

5. Click | **Add Entry** | .... **Alt** + **A**

6. Repeat steps 1–5 to add additional items.

7. Click | **Close** | .... **Alt** + **C**
   to return to document.

   To QuickCorrect words as you type:

   Select **Replace Words as You Type** ...... **Alt** + **E**

QuickCorrect Options

1. Select **Tools** .... **Alt** + **T**

2. Select **QuickCorrect** .... **Q**

3. Click | **Options...** | .... **Alt** + **O**

4. Select desired options.

5. Click | **Close** | .... **Alt** + **C**
   to return to document.

178

QUICKFINDER INDEX

A QuickFinder index is a list of every word in the files or directories you specify. A QuickFinder index is a good way to locate information quickly. It cannot be printed or viewed; however, it can only be used by the QuickFinder software to locate information.

Create QuickFinder Index

1. Select **File** menu .... **Alt**+**F**
2. Select **Open** .... **Alt**+**O**
3. Click **QuickFinder...** .... **Alt**+**F**

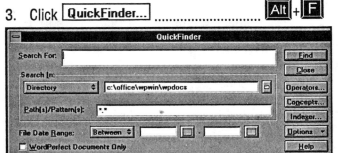

4. Select **Indexer** .... **Alt**+**X**

   If you have not previously specified directory:

   a. Specify directory .... **Alt**+**D**, *directory* for your index files.

   b. Click **OK** .... **Enter**

5. Select **Create** .... **Alt**+**R**
6. Type index name .... *index name*
7. Click **OK** .... **Enter**

continued

Create QuickFinder Index (continued)

8. Select **Browse** .... **Alt** + **W**
   to display files in current directory.

   —IN ADD DIRECTORY OR FILE BOX—

9. Indicate file or directory ... **Alt** + **D**, *file/directory*
   to index.

   *NOTE: You can use a wildcard to specify a file
   pattern.*

   To index files in all subdirectories:

   Select **Include Subtree** .... **Alt** + **N**

10. Select **Add** .... **Alt** + **A**

11. To add additional files/directories, repeat steps 8–9.

12. Select **Generate** .... **Alt** + **G**

13. Click ⌐ **OK** ⌐ .... **Enter**
    when index is complete.

14. Click ⌐ **Cancel** ⌐ .... **Esc**

15. Click ⌐ **Close** ⌐ twice .... **Alt** + **C**

Edit Index

1. Select **File** menu .... **Alt** + **F**

2. Select **Open** .... **Alt** + **O**

3. Click ⌐ **QuickFinder...** ⌐ .... **Alt** + **F**

4. Select **Indexer** .... **Alt** + **X**

continued...

Edit Index (continued)

—IN INDEX NAMES LIST—

5. Select file .... `Alt`+`N`, `↓` `↑`, `Enter`

6. Select **E**dit .... `Alt`+`E`

   To add file or directory:
   —IN ADD DIRECTORY OR FILE BOX—

   a. Enter file/directory ...... `Alt`+`D`, *file/directory*

   b. Select **A**dd .... `Alt`+`A`

   To remove file or directory:

   —IN DIRECTORIES TO INDEX BOX—

   a. Enter file/directory. `Alt`+`T`, `↓` `↑`, `Enter` to remove.

   b. Select **Re**m**o**ve .... `Alt`+`M`

7. Select **G**enerate .... `Alt`+`G`

   To update files:

   Select **U**pdate Index .... `Alt`+`U`
   with New or Modified Files.

   To regenerate all files:

   Select **I**ndex All Files .... `Alt`+`I`

8. Click [OK] .... `Enter`
   when index is complete.

9. Click [Cancel] .... `Esc`

10. Click [**C**lose] twice .... `Alt`+`C`

Update Index

1. Select **File** menu .... `Alt`+`F`

2. Select **Open** .... `Alt`+`O`

3. Click `QuickFinder...` .... `Alt`+`F`

4. Select **Indexer** .... `Alt`+`X`

   —IN INDEX NAMES BOX—

5. Select index .... `Alt`+`N`, `↓` `↑`, `Enter`
   to update.

6. Select **Edit** .... `Alt`+`E`

7. Select **Generate** .... `Alt`+`G`

8. Select **Update Index** .... `Alt`+`U`
   With New or Modified Files.

9. Click `OK` twice .... `Enter`, `Enter`

10. Click `Cancel` .... `Esc`

11. Click `Close` twice .... `Alt`+`C`

QUICKFORMAT

Copy Format of Paragraph

1. Place insertion point in paragraph containing
   format to copy.

2. Click `⬛` .... `Alt`+`R`, `Q`
   on default Toolbar.

continued...

Copy Format of Paragraph (continued)

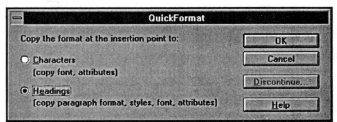

3. Choose desired option.

4. Click [OK] .... Enter

5. Drag paint roller pointer over text to format.

6. Click 🖌 .... Alt + R , Q
   on default Toolbar.

QUICKLIST

Use QuickList

1. Open dialog box containing a directory dialog box
   (e.g., Open or Save As), if one is not already open.

   NOTE: Select QuickList and Show QuickList or
   Show Both if it is not displayed.

2. Select desired item .... Alt + Q , ↓ ↑ , Enter
   from **QuickList** box.

   NOTE: If an item is a directory, double-click it to
   see a list of files for that directory.

Create/Add to QuickList

1. Open dialog box containing a directory dialog box
   (e.g., Open or Save As), if one is not already open.

   NOTE: Select QuickList and Show QuickList or
   Show Both if it is not displayed.

continued

Create/Add to QuickList (continued)

2. Select **QuickList** .... Alt + L , F4

3. Select **Add Item** ....A

   To add directory:

   —*IN DIRECTORY/FILENAME BOX*—

   Type directory .... Alt + F , *directory*

   To add document:

   —*IN DIRECTORY/FILENAME BOX*—

   Type path and filename .. Alt + F , *path/filename*

4. Type description................ Alt + D , *description*
   for information typed above in **Description** box.

5. Click OK .... Enter

6. To add other items, repeat steps 2–5.

7. Click OK .... Enter

REDLINE/STRIKEOUT

(See COMPARE DOCUMENT, page 27.)

REPLACE

(See FIND, page 60.)

REPEAT

1. Place cursor where repeated action should begin.

2. Select **Edit** menu .... Alt + E

continued...

REPEAT (continued)

3. Select **Repeat** .... Ⓐ

   —*IN NUMBER OF TIMES TO REPEAT BOX*—

4. Enter number of times .... *number*
   to repeat action.

   OR

   Accept default number of 8.

5. Click [**OK**] .... ⟦Enter⟧

6. Type keystroke.... *keystroke* or *command* or *macro*
   or select command
   or macro to repeat.

RETRIEVE DOCUMENT

To retrieve a document into a new window, use Open. (See OPEN, page 155.) To retrieve a document into the current window, use Insert.

REVEAL CODES

View Codes

1. Press **Alt+F3** .... ⟦Alt⟧+⟦F3⟧

   NOTE: To make Reveal Codes window smaller/larger, drag window dividing line down/up.

2. Move through Reveal Codes window as desired.

   NOTE: You can move the insertion point in the Reveal Codes window the same way you move through a document.

3. To hide Reveal Codes window, repeat step 1.

Delete Codes

To delete code:

Use **Backspace/Delete** keys... or

(See DELETE, page 38.)

OR

Drag code out of Reveal Codes window. *(See **Open Style Codes** and **Revertible Codes**, below, for more information.)*

Open Style Codes

*Formats your document using Initial Codes Style. This code begins each document and cannot be deleted. (See **INITIAL CODES STYLE**, page 111, for more information.)*

Revertible Codes

Appear (on either side of the selected text) as special icons, pointing to each other. When you change the formatting of selected text, you create a pair of revertible codes. When you delete one of these codes, the other one is automatically deleted.

Open Dialog Box

To change settings in codes associated with dialog boxes:

Double–click the code.

The dialog box opens and you can edit settings as usual.

Find and Replace Codes

*Helps you locate and replace codes quickly. (See **FIND**, page 60, for more information.)*

RULER BAR

Ruler Bar Appearance

- **Ruler Bar**   *Appearance varies, depending on the location of the insertion point.*

- **Document**   *For normal document text, you can drag*
  Ruler Bar   *margin markers to change the left and right margins, drag tab markers to change tab locations, drag the first line Indent marker, and drag paragraph format markers to make paragraph adjustments.*

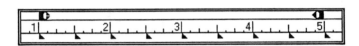

- **Column**   *For column text, you drag margin markers*
  Ruler Bar   *to reposition column margins.*

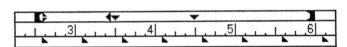

- **Table**   *For tables, you can drag margin markers to*
  Ruler Bar   *change left and right table margins. You can also drag table column markers to change column positions in the table.*

Display/Hide Ruler Bar

NOTE: *By default, the ruler bar does not display, unless you change ruler bar preferences. (See **Change Ruler Bar Preferences**, page 187.)*

Press **Alt+Shift+F3**..................................**Alt** + **Shift** + **F3**

NOTE: *To hide the ruler bar, repeat the step above.*

Change Ruler Bar Preferences

1. Select **Edit** menu .... `Alt`+`E`

2. Select **Preferences** .... `E`

3. Click Display .... `Enter`

4. Select **Ruler Bar** .... `R`

5. Choose one or more of the following options:

   - **Show Ruler Bar** .... `Alt`+`W`
     on New and Current Document

   - **Tab Snap to Ruler Bar Grid** .... `Alt`+`T`

   - **Show Ruler Bar Guides** .... `Alt`+`L`

   - **Sculptured Ruler Bar** .... `Alt`+`P`

6. Click [OK] .... `Enter`

7. Click [Close] .... `Esc`

Access Features From Ruler Bar

NOTE: *As described in the table below, you can double–click places on the ruler bar to open certain dialog boxes.*

DIALOG BOX:	DOUBLE–CLICK:
Columns	*column markers (in columns)*
Display Preferences (for ruler bar)	*non–marker areas of ruler bar (also non–margin areas)*
Margins (in text)	*margin markers (areas)*
Paragraph Format	*paragraph format markers*
Tab Set	*tab markers*
Table Format	*column or margin markers (in tables)*

SAVE

Save New Document and Continue Working

1. Press **Ctrl+S** .... `Ctrl`+`S`
2. Type filename .... *filename*
   in **Filename** text box.

   NOTE: *Indicate path to file, if necessary.*

   EXAMPLE: c:\wpwin60\wpdocs\filename

3. Click [OK] .... `Enter`

Save New Document and Exit WordPerfect

1. Press **Alt+F4**.. `Alt`+`F4`
2. Click `Yes` .... `Y`
3. Type filename .... *filename*
   in **Filename** text box.
   NOTE: Indicate path to file, if necessary.
   EXAMPLE: c:\wpwin60\wpdocs\filename
4. Click `OK` .... `Enter`

Save Document Again and Continue Working

CAUTION: *You will not be warned you are overwriting the current disk file or asked if you want to replace the file.*

Press **Ctrl+S** .... `Ctrl`+`S`

Save Document Again and Exit WordPerfect

1. Press **Alt+F4**.. `Alt`+`F4`
2. Click `Yes` .... `Y`
   to save changes.

Save Selected Text as New Document

1. Select text to save.
2. Press **Ctrl+S** .... `Ctrl`+`S`
3. Select **Selected Text** .... `S`

continued...

Save Selected Text as New Document (continued)

4. Click [OK] .... Enter

5. Type filename .... *filename*
   in **Filename** text box.

   NOTE: Indicate path to file, if necessary.

   EXAMPLE: c:\wpwin60\wpdocs\filename

6. Click [OK] .... Enter

SCREEN COLORS

(See PREFERENCES, page 170.)

SEARCH

(See FIND, page 60.)

SELECT TEXT

There are five ways to select text using the mouse. Other ways to select text, however, include Select mode keystrokes and the Select feature on the Edit menu.

Select Text Block

Drag highlight through text.

OR

1. Position cursor at beginning of text block.

2. Press **Shift** .... Shift
   and click end of desired block.

Select Word
Double–click word.

Select Sentence
Triple click any word in sentence.

OR

Click once in left margin next to sentence.

> *NOTE:* *The mouse pointer must be an arrow (not an I–beam) to use the second method.*

Select Paragraph
Click any word in paragraph four times.

OR

Double–click left margin.

> *NOTE:* *The mouse pointer must be an arrow (not an I–beam) to use the second method.*

Select to Specified Location
1. Click starting position in text.

2. Press and hold **Shift**.. `Shift`

3. Click ending position in text.

Select Text Using Select Mode Keystrokes
1. Place insertion point within text to select.

2. Press **F8** (WPWIN 6.1)................. ....`F8`
   to begin Select mode.

3. Highlight text using arrow keys.

> *EXAMPLE:* *To extend selection to the end of the line, press **End** key*

4. Make desired changes.

Select Text Using Menu

1. Place insertion point within text to select.

2. Select **Edit** menu.................................... `Alt`+`E`

3. Click **Select**... `L`

4. Choose desired option .... `↑` `↓`, `Enter`

Select Rectangular Section of Text

Selects columns of text separated by spaces.

1. Select text area from upper left corner to lower
   right corner of rectangular section.

   *NOTE: Initial selection includes column you want
   and part of all columns.*

2. Select **Edit** menu.................................... `Alt`+`E`

3. Click **Select**... `L`

4. Select **Rectangle** .... `R`

   *NOTE: Final selection includes only columns
   between upper left and lower right corners
   of initial selection.*

Select Tabular Columns

Selects columns of text separated by tabs or indents.

1. Select text area from upper left corner to lower
   right corner of tabular column.

   *NOTE: Initial selection includes column you want
   and part of all columns.*

2. Select **Edit** menu.................................... `Alt`+`E`

continued

Select Tabular Columns (continued)

3. Click **Select** L

4. Select **Tabular Column** C

> *NOTE:* *Final selection includes only columns*
> *between upper left and lower right corners*
> *of initial selection.*

Other Text Selection Methods with WPWIN 6.1 Keyboard

One character left or right...................... Shift + ← →

One line up or down............................. Shift + ↑ ↓

End of line (after codes)........................ Shift + End

Beginning of line (before codes) .... Shift + Home

Top of screen.................................... Shift + Page Up

Bottom of screen .... Shift + Page Down

First line on previous page................ Shift + Alt + Page Up

First line on next page.................... Shift + Alt + Page Up

One word left or right.................. Shift + Ctrl + ← →

One paragraph up or down .... Shift + Ctrl + ↑ ↓

Beginning of document................ Shift + Ctrl + Home
(before codes)

End of document (after codes) .... Shift + Ctrl + End

SHOW SYMBOLS

Show Symbols

Press **Ctrl+Shift+F3** .... Ctrl + Shift + F3

> *NOTE:* *To hide symbols, repeat step above.*

SORT

Arranges text alphabetically or numerically by line, paragraph, parallel columns, merge data file or table rows. Also extracts specified information from a list. The input file and output file can be the current document or a file on disk.

Sort Terms

Records	*The items to be sorted. Each record may be a line, paragraph, merge record, row of columns or a row of cells, depending on the content of the file.*
Key Definition	*Includes all components telling WordPerfect how to sort.*
Key Number	*Indicates which key WordPerfect will sort on, first, second, third, etc.*
Key Type	*Specifies whether the data is numerical or alphabetical.*
Sort Order	*Specifies whether the sort is ascending (A–Z, lowest to highest) or descending (Z–A, highest to lowest).*
Field Entry	*Specifies which tab stop or field in a merge data file to use as the sort key.*
Word Entry	*Specifies which word in the field to use as the sort key. To sort by the last word in the field, enter negative one (–1) in the text box.*
Line Entry	*Specifies which line in a record to use as the sort key.*
Cell Entry	*Specifies the cell in a table to use as the sort key.*

Sort Contents of Document

> *NOTE:* *Save document before sorting.*

1. Press **Alt+F9**..⌨Alt + ⌨F9
2. Select **Input File**...................*<Current Document>*
   or *filename.ext*

   > *NOTE:* *Tables and columns cannot be sorted to or from disk.*

3. Select **Output File**, ... ⌨Tab, *<Current Document>*
   if desired.   or *filename.ext*

4. Choose **Defined Sorts**.............⌨Alt + ⌨F, ⌨↑⌨↓
   if desired.

   To define sort key definitions:

   a. Click ⎣ **New...** ⎦ ....⌨Alt + ⌨N

   The New Sort dialog box appears.

   b. Type **Sort Name**.............................*sort name*
      if you wish to save style.

   c. Choose desired **Sort By** type...................⌨Tab

   d. Choose **Type**...........⌨Tab, ⌨Tab, ⌨F4, ⌨↑⌨↓

   e. Choose desired **Sort** ....⌨Tab, ⌨F4, ⌨↑⌨↓
      Order.

   f. Enter key position in record......⌨Tab, *number*
      (i.e., Line, Field, Word, Cell or Column).

   g. Repeat step f, as needed.

continued...

Sort Contents of Document (continued)

(See Sort Result from Sample Key Definitions, page 197.)

To add new key:

Click `Add Key` .... **Alt** + **A**

To insert new key between previous keys:

a. Position active arrow on key to precede new key.

b. Click `Insert Key` .... **Alt** + **I**

To delete key:

a. Select number of key .... **Alt** + *number*
    to delete.

b. Click `Delete Key` .... **Alt** + **D**

To specify case priority:

—FROM SORT DIALOG BOX—

NOTE: *Lowercase letters are sorted first by default.*

a. Click `Options ▾` .... **Alt** + **T**

b. Select **Uppercase First** .... **Alt** + **U**

5. Click `OK` .... **Enter**
    to sort.

6. Click `Sort` .... **Alt** + **S**

NOTES: *To sort by the last word in the field, enter negative one (–1) in the Word text box.*

*You can undo a sort with **Undo** if you do not perform any other keystrokes after obtaining the sort result.*

continued

Sort Contents of Document (continued)

EXAMPLE:

—WITH 2– AND 3–WORD FIELDS—

Sorting the list below by the second word yields inconsistent results because some of the names have two words and some have three.

Abraham Maslow
B. F. Skinner
Sigmund Freud

Therefore, the best option may be to sort this list by last word (–1), which results in a consistent order by last name:

Sigmund Freud
Abraham Maslow
B. F. Skinner

Sample Key Definitions and Description of Line Sort

Sorts records alphabetically by the first word in Field 1 of Line 1. In the event of identical data or words, WordPerfect looks at the second word in Field 1. If this is also identical, WordPerfect looks at the first word in Field 2.

KEY	TYPE	FIELD	LINE	WORD
1	Alpha	1	1	1
2	Alpha	1	1	2
3	Alpha	2	1	1

Sort Result from Sample Key Definitions

In the following example, each line is a record. Each field is separated by a tab, and each record ends with a hard return.

continued…

Sort Result from Sample Key Definitions (continued)

FIELD 1	FIELD 2	FIELD 3	FIELD 4	FIELD 5
Knappen	Robyn	470 Athens Ave.	Skaville	IL 60513
Mar	Steve	934 Hillegass	Berkeley	CA 94702
Roche	Cindy	123 St. Olaf Ave.	Northfield	MN 55057
Scilingo	Denise	25 Stein Way	Milwaukee	WI 53211
Smith	David F.	1 Archbishop	Sacramento	CA 95816

Select Records

Extracts records meeting specified criteria, with or without sorting. The output file contains only the records selected by the specified criteria.

> CAUTION: Save document before selecting records.

1. Press **Alt+F9** .... **Alt**+**F9**

2. Select **Input File** ....<Current Document>
   or *filename.ext.*

   > NOTE: Tables and columns cannot be sorted to or from disk.

3. Select **Output File** ....<Current Document>
   or *filename.ext.*

4. Select type of record to sort by.

5. Define sort keys following **Sort Contents of Document** procedure, page 195.

6. Place insertion point .... **Alt**+**R**
   in **Select Records** text box.

7. Type selection statement ....*text*
   in text box using operators visible in status bar.

continued

Select Records (continued)

EXAMPLE: key3=Milwaukee | key3=Northfield

This selection statement isolates records with Milwaukee or Northfield for key 3.

(See Selection Statement—Operators and Examples, below.)

> *NOTE:* Click **Se̲lect Without Sorting** check box if you do not want to sort extracted records.

8. Click [**OK**] .... |Enter|

9. Click [**Sort**] .... |Alt|+|S|

> *NOTES:* Only records meeting selection criteria appear in the output file.
>
> You can undo a sort with **Undo** if you do not perform any other keystrokes after obtaining the sort result.

Selection Statement—Operators and Examples

Use the following operators and examples as a guide for entering a selection statement (see step 8, Select Records, above) to extract desired records.

OPERATORS: DESCRIPTION:

| Selects records meeting conditions of either key (an OR condition).

EXAMPLE: key3=Milwaukee | key3=Northfield

> *Selects records that have Milwaukee or Northfield for key 3.*

continued...

Selection Statement (continued)

OPERATORS: **DESCRIPTION:**

& Selects records meeting conditions of both records (an AND condition).

EXAMPLE: key1=Scilingo & key3=Milwaukee
Selects records that have Scilingo for key 1 and Milwaukee for key 3.

= Selects records exactly matching condition of statement.

EXAMPLE: key1=Scilingo
Selects records that have Scilingo for key 1.

<> Selects records that do not equal condition of statement.

EXAMPLE: key1<>Scilingo
Selects records that do not have Scilingo for key 1.

> Selects records with a value greater than the condition of the statement.

EXAMPLE: key6>500
Selects records with a key 6 value greater than 500.

< Selects records with a value less than the condition of the statement.

EXAMPLE: key6<500
Selects records with a key 6 value less than 500.

>= Selects records with a value greater than or equal to the condition of the statement.

EXAMPLE: key6>=500
Selects records with a key 6 value greater than or equal to 500.

continued.

Selection Statement (continued)

OPERATORS: **DESCRIPTION:**

<=   Selects records with a value less than or equal to the condition of the statement.

EXAMPLE: key6<=500

> *Selects records with a key 6 value less than or equal to 500.*

SPECIAL CODES

(See OTHER CODES, page 155.)

SPELL CHECKER

1. Place insertion point in document to check.

2. Click 🖺 .... `Ctrl`+`F1`
   on default Toolbar.

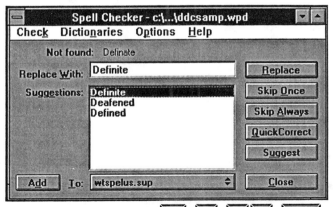

3. Select **Che<u>c</u>k** menu..... `Alt`+`K`, `↑` `↓`, `Enter`
   to specify part of document to check.

continued...

SPELL CHECKER (continued)

4. Select **Dictionaries** .... `Alt`+`N`, `↑``↓`, `Enter`
   menu to choose dictionary to add
   words to, if desired.

   NOTE: *The filename of the main dictionary is*
   wp{wp}us.lex. Supplementary dictionaries
   have a file extension of .sup. (See
   ***LOCATION OF FILES**, page 135, for default*
   location of dictionary files.)

5. Select **Options** menu . `Alt`+`P`, `↑``↓`, `Enter`
   to choose desired options.

6. Click `    Start    ` .... `Alt`+`S`

7. Choose desired button option when Spell Checker
   stops and highlights a word.

8. Click `    Close    ` .... `Esc`
   to return to document.

SPREADSHEET/DATABASE IMPORT AND LINK

Import or Link Spreadsheet/Database

1. Place cursor where information is to appear.

2. Select **Insert** menu .... **Alt** + **I**

3. Select **Spreadsheet/Database** .... **R**

4. Select **Import** .... **I**

   OR

   Select **Create Link** .... **C**

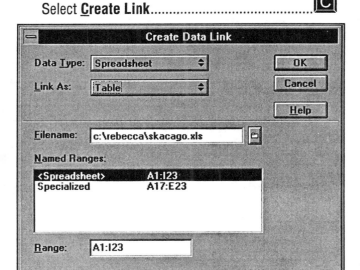

5. Select desired .... **Alt** + **T**, **F4**, **↑** **↓**, **Enter**
   Data Type.

continued...

Import or Link Spreadsheet/Database (continued)

6. Select desired .... Alt + I, F4, ↑ ↓, Enter
   Import As format.

   OR

   Select desired .... Alt + L, F4, ↑ ↓, Enter
   Link As format.

7. Select/type desired **Filename** .... Tab, *filename*
   in text box.

   *NOTE: Click [icon] to access **Select File** dialog box.*

   EXAMPLE: C:\123R4\BUDG94.WKS

   To limit import or link to range in spreadsheet:

   a. Select **Named Ranges** list box .... Alt + N
   b. Select desired named range .... ↑ ↓

   OR

   a. Select **Range** text box .... Alt + R
   b. Enter desired cell range........................... *range*

   EXAMPLE: A1:B20

8. Click OK .... Enter
   to insert into document.

   NOTE: Link icons appear in the left margin of document at beginning and end of linked data.

Edit Spreadsheet/Database Link

1. Place insertion point between link icons.

   NOTE: A link information box containing name of linked file appears.

2. Select **I**nsert menu .... `Alt`+`I`

3. Select **Sp**r**eadsheet/Database** .... `R`

4. Select **E**dit Link .... `E`

5. Choose feature to edit *(see **Import or Link Spreadsheet/Database**, steps 5–9, page 203).*

6. Click `OK` .... `Enter`

Update Spreadsheet/Database Links

1. Place insertion point anywhere in document.

2. Select **I**nsert menu .... `Alt`+`I`

3. Select **Sp**r**eadsheet/Database** .... `R`

4. Select **U**pdate .... `U`

5. Click `Yes` .... `Y`
   to update all data links.

Use Spreadsheet/Database Options

1. Place insertion point anywhere in document.

2. Select **I**nsert menu .... `Alt`+`I`

3. Select **Sp**r**eadsheet/Database** .... `R`

continued...

Use Spreadsheet/Database Options (continued)

4. Select **O**ptions .... O

5. Select/deselect desired option(s).

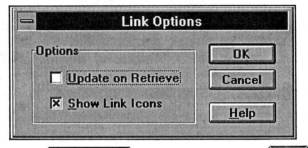

6. Click [OK] .... Enter

STYLES

Create Style in Style Editor

NOTE: When you create a style, it is saved with current document only.

1. Click 🔳 .... Alt + F8
   on Format Toolbar.

2. Click [C**r**eate...] .... Alt + R

3. Type style name .... *name*
   in **St**yle Name text box.

4. Type style description .... Tab, *description*
   in **D**escription text box.

5. Select desired ...... Alt + Y, F4, ↑, ↓, Enter
   T**y**pe option.

continued

Create Style in Style Editor (continued)

6. Specify **Enter** key action in character styles or paragraph styles:

   To have Enter insert hard return, leaving style on:

   Deselect **E**n**ter Key will Chain to**............ Alt + N

   To have Enter turn style off, then on again:

   a. Select **E**n**ter Key will Chain to**......... Alt + N

   b. Select **<Same Style>** .... Tab , F4 , ↑ ↓

   To have Enter turn style off and leave it off:

   a. Select **E**n**ter Key will Chain to**......... Alt + N

   b. Select **<None>** .. .. Tab , F4 , ↑ ↓
      from drop–down list.

   To have Enter turn style off/turn on new style:

   a. Select **E**n**ter Key will Chain to**......... Alt + N

   b. Select desired style .... Tab , F4 , ↑ ↓
      from drop–down list.

7. Click [**OK**] .... Enter

8. Click [**Apply**] .... Alt + A
   to use style immediately.

   OR

   Click [**Close**] .... Esc
   to return to document.

Create Style from Existing Text

1. Place insertion point in preformatted text.

2. Click `ᴨ¶ / àà` .... `Alt`+`F8`
   on Format Toolbar.

3. Click `QuickStyle...` .... `Alt`+`Q`

4. Type style name....................................*style name*
   in **Style Name** text box.

5. Type description .... `Tab`, *description*
   in **Description** text box.

6. Select desired **Style Type** option.

7. Click `OK` .... `Enter`

8. Apply style *(see below)* or close **Style List** dialog
   box, as desired.

Apply Style to Text

Applies style to selected text or to document after insertion point.

1. Place insertion point where style is to begin:

   - **Paragraph style**   *Place anywhere in paragraph.*

   - **Character style**   *Select text to format.*

   - **Document style**   *Place where formatting is to begin.*

2. Click `ᴨ¶ / àà` .... `Alt`+`F8`
   on Format Toolbar.

continued

Apply Style to Text (continued)

3. Click `Options ▼` .... `Alt`+`O`, `F4`

4. Select **Setup** .... `Alt`+`S`

5. Select desired **Display Files From** options.

6. Select desired **Default Location** option.

7. Click `OK` .... `Enter`

8. Select desired style .... `Alt`+`N`, `↑` `↓`
   from **Name** list.

9. Click `Apply` .... `Enter`

Edit Style

1. Click `¶` .... `Alt`+`F8`
   on Format Toolbar.

2. Select style .... `↑` `↓`
   to edit from **Name** list.

3. Click `Edit...` .... `Alt`+`E`

4. Change desired features *(see steps 5–8, **Create
   Style in Style Editor**, page 206)*.

5. Click `OK` .... `Enter`

6. Click `Apply` .... `Enter`

   OR

   Click `Close` .... `Esc`
   to return to document.

Retrieve Styles into Current Document

1. Click 𝄆ᵃᵃ𝄇 .... **Alt**+**F8**
   on Format Toolbar.

2. Click **Options ▼** .... **Alt**+**O**, **F4**

3. Select **R‍etrieve** .... **E**

4. Type style filename .... *filename*
   in **F‍ilename** text box,
   or select from drop–down list.

   NOTE: To access drop–down list, click ▭

5. Click **OK** .... **Enter**

6. Click **Close** .... **Esc**
   to return to document.

Delete Style in Document

To delete individual occurrences of style:

Delete `Para Style: name ⟩` and/or `⟨ Para Style: name`
or `Open Style: InitialStyle` from Reveal Codes screen.
*(See **DELETE CODES**, page 38.)*

To delete style throughout document:

a. Click 𝄆ᵃᵃ𝄇 .... **Alt**+**F8**
   on Format Toolbar.

b. Select style .... **↑** **↓**
   to delete in list box.

c. Click **Options ▼** .... **Alt**+**O**, **F4**

continued

Delete Style in Document (continued)

d. Click ⸝Delete...⸝ .... D

e. Select **Include Codes**............................... I
   to delete style and formatting.

   OR

   Select **Leave Codes** L
   to delete style but leave
   formatting in document.

f. Click ⸝ OK ⸝ .... Enter

g. Click ⸝ Close ⸝ .... Esc
   to return to document.

Save Styles for Use in Other Documents

NOTE: The complete list of styles is saved as a separate style file.

1. Click ⸝⸝ .... Alt + F8
   on Format Toolbar.

2. Click ⸝Options ▾⸝ .... Alt + O , F4

3. Select **Save As** .... A

4. Type style filename....................................*filename*
   in **Filename** text box, or select from list.

   NOTE: To access drop-down list, click ⸝⸝

5. Select desired **Style Type** option.

6. Click ⸝ OK ⸝ .... Enter

7. Click ⸝ Close ⸝ .... Esc

Create Graphics Style

1. Select **Graphics** .... `Alt`+`G`

2. Select **Graphics Styles** .... `G`

3. Select desired **Style Type** option.

4. Select desired **Styles** type from list box.

5. Click `Create...` .... `Alt`+`R`

6. Type style filename .... *filename*
   in **Filename** text box, or select from list.

   NOTE: To access drop-down list, click 🗀

7. Select desired options for style type (box style,
   border style, line style, fill style).

   (See GRAPHICS, page 76.)

8. Click `OK` .... `Enter`

9. Click `Close` .... `Esc`
   to return to document.

Edit Graphics Style

1. Select **Graphics** .... `Alt`+`G`

2. Select **Graphics Styles** .... `G`

3. Select desired **Style Type** option.

4. Select style .... `↑``↓`
   to edit from **Styles** list.

continued

Edit Graphics Style (continued)

5. Click [**Edit...**] .... `Alt`+`E`

6. Select desired options for style type (box style, border style, line style, fill style).

    (See GRAPHICS—EDIT, page 84.)

7. Click [**OK**] .... `Enter`

8. Click [**Close**] .... `Esc`
    to return to document.

Copy Graphics Styles to Default or Supplemental Template

1. Select **Graphics** .... `Alt`+`G`

2. Select **Graphics Styles** .... `G`

3. Select desired **Style Type** .... `Alt`+`S`, `↑` `↓`
    option and **Styles** to copy.

4. Click [Options ▼] .... `Alt`+`O`, `F4`

5. Select **Copy** .... `C`

6. Type style name .... *style name*
    in **New Style Name** text box.

7. Click [**OK**] .... `Enter`

8. Click [**Close**] .... `Esc`

214

Retrieve Graphics Styles

1. Select **Graphics** .... Alt + G

2. Select **Graphics Styles** .... G

3. Select desired **Style Type** .... Alt + S , ↑ ↓
    option and **Styles** to retrieve.

4. Click Options ▼ .... Alt + O , F4

5. Select **Retrieve** .... E

6. Type graphics style filename .... *filename*
    in **Filename** text box,
    or select from drop–down list.

    NOTES: To access drop–down list, click 🗁

    Type path, if necessary.

    EXAMPLE: c:\wpwin60\graphics\ourlogo.wpg

7. Click OK .... Enter

8. Click Close .... Esc

Delete Graphics Styles

1. Select **Graphics** .... Alt + G

2. Select **Graphics Styles** .... G

3. Select desired **Style Type** .... Alt + S , ↑ ↓
    option and **Styles** to delete.

4. Click Options ▼ .... Alt + O , F4

continued.

Delete Graphics Styles (continued)

5. Select **Delete**... D

6. Click **Yes** .... Y
   to confirm deletion.

7. Click **Close** .... Esc

   NOTE: *Graphics styles are saved in current*
   document or default template unless you
   choose a different location from the
   ***Options** button, **Setup** pop–up list. The*
   most common place to save them is to a
   template.

SUBDIVIDE PAGE

1. Place insertion point in page to subdivide.

2. Click ⊞ .... Alt + R , P , V
   on Page Toolbar.

The Subdivide Page dialog box appears.

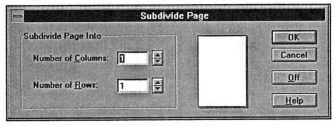

3. Enter number of columns...........................*number*
   in **Number of Columns** text box.

continued...

SUBDIVIDE PAGE (continued)

4. Type number of rows.....................⬛Tab⬛, *number*
   in **Number of Rows** text box.

5. Click ⬛ OK ⬛ .... ⬛Enter⬛

   To turn off subdivide page:

   a. Place cursor where subdivision is to end.

   b. Click ⬛⊞⬛ .... ⬛Alt⬛+⬛R⬛, ⬛P⬛, ⬛V⬛
      on Page Toolbar.

   c. Click ⬛ Off ⬛ .... ⬛Alt⬛+⬛O⬛

Move Between Logical Pages

To end text typed on logical page/move to next:

Press **Ctrl+Enter**.............................⬛Ctrl⬛+⬛Enter⬛

To move to next or previous logical page:

Press **Alt+PgUp/PgDn**.................⬛Alt⬛+⬛Page Up⬛/⬛Page Down⬛

To move directly to specified page:

a. Press **Ctrl+G**.................................⬛Ctrl⬛+⬛G⬛

b. Enter **Page Number** .... *number*

c. Click ⬛ OK ⬛ .... ⬛Enter⬛

Print Subdivided Pages as Booklet

1. Click ⬛▤⬛........................... ⬛Alt⬛+⬛R⬛, ⬛P⬛, ⬛S⬛
   on Page Toolbar.

continued.

Print Subdivided Pages as Booklet (continued)

2. Select or create desired paper size. *(See **PAPER SIZE**, page 164.)*

3. Click <u>Select</u> .... `Enter`

4. Click 📖 .... `Alt`+`R`, `P`, `I`
   on Page Toolbar.

5. Choose desired **Binding** .... `Tab`, *number*
   Width options.

6. Choose desired.. `Alt`+`D`, `F4`, `↑` `↓`, `Enter`
   Print Options.

7. Click <u>OK</u> .... `Enter`

8. Click 🔲 .... `Alt`+`R`, `P`, `V`
   on Page Toolbar.

9. Enter *2*... `2`
   in **Number of Columns** text box.

10. Enter *1*... `Tab`, `1`
    in **Number of Rows** text box.

11. Click <u>OK</u> .... `Enter`

12. Type text and enter graphics, as desired.

13. Click 🖨 .... `Ctrl`+`P`

14. Select **Multiple Pages**................................ `M`

continued...

Print Subdivided Pages as Booklet (continued)

15. Click `Options...` .... O

16. Select **Booklet Printing** check box.................. B

17. Click `OK` .... Enter

18. Click `Print` .... Enter

19. Enter desired **Print Range** .... *page numbers*

20. Click `Print...` .... Enter

SUPPRESS

1. Place insertion point at top of page.

2. Click 🗒 .... Alt + R , P , U
   on Page Toolbar.

3. Choose item(s) to suppress from listed options.

To print current page number at bottom center of
page:

Select **Print Page Number** .... Alt + N
at Bottom Center on Current Page check box.

4. Click `OK` .... Enter

TABLE OF AUTHORITIES

Creates a table containing lists of citations. The table can be divided into one or more sections (e.g., Cases, Constitutional Provisions, Statutory Provisions, etc.). The citations within each section are sorted alphanumerically.

To create a table of authorities, you must complete the following four steps:

1. *Define the sections of your table.*

2. *Mark items to include in table of authorities.*

3. *Define table of authorities style and location.*

4. *Generate the table of authorities.*

All these procedures are described below.

Mark Citations

Allows you to mark citations in text, captions, endnotes, footnotes and graphics boxes. The first time you mark text for an authority, you create the long form of the authority.

This procedure allows you to check the authority as it will appear in the table. It also assigns a short form or nickname to the authority. Then, when you mark later text for the authority, you use the short form.

Define Table of Authorities Section

1. Place insertion point where section is to appear.

2. Type a title.. *title*
   (e.g., Cases), if desired.

3. Press **Enter**.. Enter
   for spacing, as desired.

continued…

220

Define Table of Authorities Section (continued)

To display Table of Authorities feature bar:
Click ⚖ .... **Alt**+**T**, **A**

on Generate Toolbar.

Table of Authorities feature bar appears.

| ? Short Form: | ± | Mark | Create Full Form... | Edit Full Form... | Define... | Close | Generate... |

4. Click **Define...** .... **Shift**+**Alt**+**D**

5. Create, edit or retrieve a section definition *(see **Create/Edit Section**, below).*

6. Select the section.

7. Click **Insert** .... **Alt**+**I**

8. Repeat steps above for each section.

<<Table of Authorities will generate here>> appears.

Create/Edit Section

Creates different sections in a table (e.g., cases).

> —*WITH TABLE OF AUTHORITIES FEATURE BAR ACTIVE*—

1. Click **Define...** .... **Shift**+**Alt**+**D**

2. Do one of the following:

   a. Click **Create...** .... **Alt**+**A**

   b. Type section name .... *section name*

   OR

   a. Select section to edit .... **↑** **↓**

   b. Click **Edit...** .... **Alt**+**E**

continued

To position and format for page numbers:

a. Select **Page Numbering**.................. `Alt`+`G`

b. Select **Document Page** ....`D`
   Number Format to return
   to document page number format.

c. Click `OK` .... `Enter`

If you want underlining in marked text to appear in table:

Select **Underlining** .... `Alt`+`U`
Allowed check box.

To see each number printed (e.g., 20, 21, 22) instead of combined (e.g., 20–22):

Select/deselect **Use Dash to Show**........ `Alt`+`D`
Consecutive Pages check box

3. Click `Use as Default` .... `Alt`+`A`
   to save new selections
   as default settings.

4. Click `OK` .... `Enter`

5. Click `Insert` .... `Enter`

Retrieve Section

Retrieves section definitions from another document.

—WITH TABLE OF AUTHORITIES FEATURE
BAR ACTIVE—

1. Click `Define...` .... **Shift** + **Alt** + **D**

2. Click `Retrieve...` .... **Alt** + **R**

3. Type name of document .... *filename*
   containing section definitions,
   or select desired one.

   *NOTE: To access **Select File** dialog box,*
   click 🗀

4. Select desired .... **Tab**, **↑** **↓**, **Enter**
   definition(s).

5. Click `    OK    ` .... **Enter**

Mark First Occurrence of Citation—
Full Form

NOTE: Use this procedure the first time you mark
for a citation. After this first time, the
*short form of the procedure, **Mark***
Subsequent Occurrences of Citation—
Short Form, below, can be used.

—WITH TABLE OF AUTHORITIES FEATURE
BAR ACTIVE—

1. Select text to mark.

2. Click `Create Full Form...` .... **Shift** + **Alt** + **R**

continued

Mark First Occurrence of Citation Full Form (cont)

3. Type **Section Name**.. *name*
   or select desired one.

   *NOTE: To access **Select File** dialog box, click* 🗀

4. Edit text in the **Short Form** .... **Tab**
   text box, if desired.
   *NOTE: A unique short form name should be
   assigned for every full form.*

5. Click [**OK**] ....**Enter**

6. Edit full form text so it appears as desired in table.

7. Click [**Close**] .... **Shift** + **Alt** + **C**

Mark Subsequent Occurrences of Citation—Short Form

*NOTE: Use this procedure to mark occurrences
after the first occurrence. For first
occurrences, use the full form procedure,
**Mark First Occurrence of Citation–Full
Form**, above.*

*—WITH TABLE OF AUTHORITIES FEATURE
BAR ACTIVE—*

1. Select text to mark.

2. Type short .... **Shift** + **Alt** + **S** , *name*
   form name or select desired one.

   *NOTE   To access **Select File** dialog box, click* 🗀

3. Click [**Mark**] .... **Shift** + **Alt** + **M**

4. Repeat steps 1–3 for each occurrence of citation.

Define Table of Authorities Section

*—WITH TABLE OF AUTHORITIES FEATURE
BAR ACTIVE—*

1. Place insertion point where section is to appear.

2. Type a title ....*title*
    (e.g., Cases), if desired.

3. Press **Enter** .... `Enter`

4. Click `Define...` .... `Shift`+`Alt`+`D`

5. Create, edit or retrieve section definition.

6. Select the section.

7. Click `Insert` .... `Alt`+`I`

8. Repeat above steps for each section.

Generate Table of Authorities

*—WITH TABLE OF AUTHORITIES FEATURE
BAR ACTIVE—*

1. Click `Generate...` .... `Shift`+`Alt`+`G`

2. Click `OK` .... `Enter`

(See GENERATE, page 72, for more information.)

TABLE OF CONTENTS

Complete the following three steps to create a table of contents:

1. *Mark items to include in table of contents.*

2. *Define table of contents style and location.*

3. *Generate the table of contents.*

All these procedures are described below.

Mark Table of Contents Text

To display Table of Contents feature bar:

Click 🖼 .... **Alt**+**T**, **C**

The Table of Contents feature bar appears.

| **?** Table of Contents Level: | Mark 1 | Mark 2 | Mark 3 | Mark 4 | Mark 5 | Define... | Close | Generate... |

1. Select word(s) to include in table of contents.

2. Select **Mark X**............................ **Shift**+**Alt**+**#**
   (where X is the level number
   you are marking) to indicate
   level to mark.

3. Repeat steps 1–2 for every entry to add to table of
   contents.

4. Click [**Close**] .... **Shift**+**Alt**+**C**
   to return to document.

Define Table of Contents

*—WITH TABLE OF CONTENTS FEATURE
BAR ACTIVE—*

1. Place cursor where table of contents is to appear.

2. Type a title.. *title*
   (e.g., Table of Contents), if desired.

3. Press **Enter**... **Enter**
   for spacing, as desired.

4. Click [Define...] .... **Shift**+**Alt**+**D**

continued...

Define Table of Contents (continued)

5. Enter desired number of levels .... *number*

6. Select **Level #** .... Alt +# , F4
    to choose desired
    page numbering position.

7. Choose desired option .... ↑ ↓

    **If creating table of contents with more than one
    level, the last level wrapped flush left (instead of
    indented):**

    Select **Display Last Level** .... Alt +D
    in Wrapped Format check box.

    *NOTE: If you choose the option above, only the
    first three numbering formats are available
    for the last level. Also, all last level
    headings appear one after the other on the
    same line. If all the entries are longer than
    one line, the remaining text wraps.*

8. Click OK .... Enter

<<Table of Contents will generate here>> appears.

Generate Table of Contents

—WITH TABLE OF CONTENTS FEATURE
BAR ACTIVE—

1. Click `Generate...` .... `Shift`+`Alt`+`G`

The Generate dialog box appears.

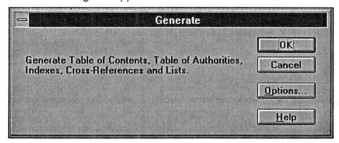

If you are generating a table of contents for a master document and want to save generated subdocuments:

a. Click `Options...` .... `O`

b. Select **Save Subdocuments** .... `S`

c. Click `OK` .... `Enter`

If you are generating a table of contents for a document containing hypertext links and want to create links:

a. Click `Options...` .... `O`

b. Select **Build Hypertext Links** .... `B`

c. Click `OK` .... `Enter`

continued...

228

Generate Table of Contents (continued)

2. Click [　OK　]

3. Click [　**Close**　] .... Shift + Alt + C

(See GENERATE, page 72, for more information.)

TABLES

Create Table

Click [Tables ▼] on power bar and select desired number of rows/columns.

OR

1. Press **F12** F12

2. Type number of columns .... *number*
   in **Columns** text box.

3. Type number of rows.................. Tab, *number*
   select **Rows** text box.

4. Click [　OK　] .... Enter

Convert Tabular or Parallel Columns to a Table

1. Select columns to convert.

2. Press **F12** F12

   If selected text columns are tabular:

   Select **Tabular Column**.......................... T

   If selected text columns are parallel:

   Select **Parallel Column** .... P

continued

Convert Tabular/Parallel Columns to Table (cont)

NOTE: *Newspaper style columns are not parallel columns. If newspaper columns are used to create a table, each column entry creates a separate table 1X1.*

3. Click `OK` .... `Enter`

Insertion Point Movement in Tables

Next cell right...................................... `Tab`

Previous cell left .... `Shift`+`Tab`

Up or Down one cell .... `Alt`+`↑` `↓`

First cell in row .... `Home`, `Home`

Last cell in row............................. `End`, `End`

Top line of cell .... `Alt`+`Home`

Bottom line of cell .... `Alt`+`End`

Insert Tab in Table Cells

NOTE: *Because **Tab** moves insertion point to next cell, a hard tab must be used to insert a tab in a cell. (See **OTHER CODES**, page 155.)*

Hard Left Tab

Press **Ctrl+Tab**............................. `Ctrl`+`Tab`

Hard Decimal Tab

Press **Alt+Shift+F7** .... `Alt`+`Shift`+`F7`

continued...

Insert Tab in Table Cells (continued)

Hard Back Tab

Press **Ctrl+Shift+Tab** ....

Select Table Cells Using Mouse

> *NOTE:*   *When cells are selected, the text in the*
> *cells is also selected, and you can use*
> *table structure or table format settings.*

Select One Cell
1.   Place insertion point just below horizontal line or just to right of vertical line in cell to select.

Insertion point becomes a white arrow ▷

2.   Click mouse button.

Select All Cells in Column
1.   Place insertion point just below horizontal line in column to select.

Insertion point becomes a white arrow ▷

2.   Double–click mouse button.

Select All Cells in Row
1.   Place insertion point just to right of any cell in row to select.

Insertion point becomes a white arrow ▷

2.   Double–click mouse button.

Select All Cells in Table
1.   Place insertion point just below horizontal line or just to right of vertical line in cell to select.

Insertion point becomes a white arrow ▷

2.   Triple click mouse button.

Deselect All Cells in Table
Click any cell.

Move or Copy Cells, Rows or Columns

1. Select desired cells, rows or columns.

2. Click ✂ .... Ctrl + X

   OR

   Click 📋 .... Ctrl + C

3. Select **S**election .... S
   to cut or copy cells and contents.

   OR

   Select **R**ow .... R
   to cut or copy entire row and contents.

   OR

   Select **C**olumn C
   to cut or copy entire column and contents.

   OR

   a. Select C**e**ll .... E
      to copy only one cell.

   b. Select **D**own or R**i**ght .... D or I

   c. Enter number of cells down .... *number*
      or right to move data.

4. Click 🔲 **OK** 🔲 .... Enter

5. Place insertion point in cell to receive cut or copied selection.

6. Click 📋 .... Ctrl + V

Insert Rows/Columns in Table

1. Place insertion point in table where rows or columns are to appear.

2. Select **Table** menu.................................. `Alt`+`A`

3. Select **Insert** .... `I`

4. Enter number of **Row(s)** .... `Tab`, *number*
   to insert in text box.

   OR

   Select **Column(s)**.............................. `C`, *number*
   and enter number of columns
   to insert in text box.

5. Select **Placement, Before** .... `Alt`+`B`
   current column or row.

   OR

   Select **Placement, After** .... `Alt`+`A`

6. Click `OK` .... `Enter`

   *NOTE: To insert one row quickly, press **Alt+Ins**.
   To delete current row quickly, press
   Alt+Del.*

Delete Rows/Columns (Structure or Text)

1. Place insertion point in column or row to delete, or select all desired cells.

continued

Delete Rows/Columns (continued)

2. Right–click mouse button .... *click*, **D**
   and select **Delete**.

   > *NOTE:* *If you selected cells to delete, you don't*
   > *need to complete steps 3–4; go directly to*
   > *step 5.*

3. Enter number of **Row(s)**................... **Tab**, *number*
   to delete in text box.

   OR

   Select **Column(s)** .... **C**, *number*
   and enter number of columns
   to delete in text box.

   To delete text only:

   Select **Cell Contents**................................. **E**
   (text or formulas).

4. Click [**OK**] .... **Enter**

   > *NOTE:* *To restore deleted column or row with*
   > *contents, see **UNDO**, page 260.*

Delete Table

Deletes entire table (structure and text), only the table structure,
or only the table text.

1. Select table.

2. Right–click mouse button .... *click*, **D**
   and select **Delete**.

continued...

Delete Table (continued)

3. Select desired option *(see below)*.

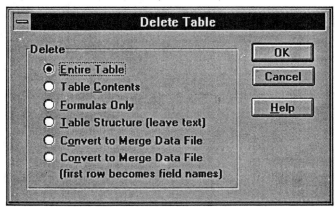

4. Click [OK] .... Enter

Adjust Horizontal Table Position

1. Place insertion point in table.

2. Click 🖫 .... Ctrl + F12
   on Table Toolbar.

4. Select **Table** .... Alt + A

5. Choose desired .... *click*, F4, ↑ ↓ , Enter
   position from **Table**
   Position pop–up list
   at bottom left of window.

continued

Adjust Horizontal Table Position (continued)

To place table specified distance from left edge of page:

a. Select **From Left Edge** .... 🇪

b. Enter distance (inches) .... Tab, *number* from left edge of page in text box.

6. Click [OK] .... Enter

Change Table Size and Column Width Using Ruler Bar

1. Place insertion point in table.

   To display ruler bar (if necessary):

   Press **Alt+Shift+F3** .... Alt + Shift + F3

2. Drag table margin markers ⫣ and column width markers ⫤ to desired locations on ruler bar.

Format Table Borders/Lines

Tables have three kinds of lines: Table Border, Table Lines (lines outside a selected rectangle of cells) and Table Lines (lines inside a selected rectangle of cells).

1. Place insertion point in table, or select desired cells.

2. Click 🗒 .... Shift + F12 on Table Toolbar.

   To format table border:

   a. Select **Table** .... Ⓐ

continued...

Format Table Borders/Lines (continued)

b. Select **B**order .... `Alt`+`B`, `Tab`, `F4`

c. Select desired border style............... `↑` `↓`
from drop–down list.

To format lines outside selected cells:

a. Select **Each S**elected Cell...................... `S`

b. Choose each **Line**................... `Tab`, `Tab`, `F4`
Style format.

c. Select desired line style................... `↑` `↓`
from drop–down list
for each line to format.

To format lines inside selected cells:

a. Select **Sele**c**tion**..................................... `C`
if not preselected.

b. Select **I**nside .... `Alt`+`I`, `Tab`, `F4`
to format inside lines.

*NOTE: The **I**nside option is not available unless
more than one cell is selected.*

c. Select desired line style................... `↑` `↓`
from drop–down list.

3. Click [OK   ] .... `Enter`

Turn Off Table Lines

1. Place insertion point in table, or select desired cells.

2. Click 🔲 .... **Shift** + **F12**
   on Table Toolbar.

3. Select desired option.

4. Select lines .... **Tab**, **Tab**, **F4**, **↑** **↓**
   to turn off from pop–up list.

5. Click **OK** .... **Enter**

Fill Current Cell or Selection

1. Place insertion point in cell, or select desired cells.

2. Click 🔲 .... **Shift** + **F12**
   on Table Toolbar.

3. Select desired option.

4. Select **Fill Style** palette .... **Alt** + **F**, **Tab**, **F4**

5. Choose desired pattern .... **↑** **↓**

   NOTE: Shading and percent of shading are also selected here.

6. If desired, select **Foreground** and **Background** colors from palettes.

   NOTE: You must use a mouse for step above.

7. Click **OK** .... **Enter**

238

Join Cells/Tables

Combines two or more cells/tables.

To join cells:
Select cells to join. *(See **Select Table Using Mouse**, page 230.)*

To join table:
a.   Place tables directly above/below one another.

CAUTION: Move any text appearing between tables out of the way!

b.   Delete Hard Return codes `HRt` between Table Off codes `Tbl Off` in first table and Table Definition codes `Tbl Def` in second table.

c.   Place insertion point anywhere in first table.

1.   Select **Ta̲ble** menu .... `Alt`+`A`

2.   Select **J̲oin** .... `J`

3.   Select **C̲ell** .... `C`

   OR

   Select **T̲able** .... `T`
   NOTE: Format of first table is applied to second table, except in individually formatted cells.

Split Cell/Table
   —WITH REVEAL CODES ON—

1.   Place cursor in table at desired split location.

continued

Split Cell/Table (continued)

2. Select **Ta̲ble** menu .... Alt + A

3. Select **S̲plit**... S

    To split cell:

    a. Select **C̲ell** C

    b. Select and enter **Columns**.......... Tab, *number*
        OR
        Select and enter **R̲ows** .... R, *number*

    c. Click ⌈ **OK** ⌉ .... Enter

    To split table:

    a. Select **T̲able**. .... T

    b. Place insertion point between Table Off Tbl Off
        and Table Definition Tbl Def codes.

    c. Enter several HRt ...... Enter, Enter, Enter
        to separate tables.

Cell Text Size/Appearance

Formats the size and appearance of text in specified cells automatically. (See Table Column Text Size/Appearance, page 239.)

1. Place insertion point in cell to format, or select desired cells.

2. Click 🖮 .... Ctrl + F12
    on Table Toolbar.

continued...

Cell Text Size/Appearance (continued)

3. Select **Cell** .... E

4. Choose desired **Appearance** options......... *letter(s)*

   To change position of text in cells:

   a. Select **Position**............................... P , F4

   b. Choose desired .... ↑ ↓ , Enter
      position option.

   To change size of text in cells:

   a. Select **Size** .... Alt + Z , F4

   b. Choose desired option .... ↑ ↓ , Enter

5. Click ▭ OK ▭ .... Enter

Vertically Align Text in Cells

1. Place cursor in cell to format, or select cells to
   format.

2. Click 🖮 ....Ctrl + F12
   on Table Toolbar.

3. Select **Cell** .... E

4. Select **Vertical Alignment** .... V , F4

5. Choose desired .... ↑ ↓ , Enter
   alignment option.

6. Click ▭ OK ▭ .... Enter

   NOTE: *You must view the document in Page*
   mode to see the new alignment.

Lock or Unlock Cells

Lock cells to prevent text inside them from being altered.   (See Disable/Enable Cell Locking, below.)

1. Place insertion point in cell to (un)lock, or select desired cell.

2   Click 🖮 .... `Ctrl`+`F12`
    on Table Toolbar.

3. Select **C<u>e</u>ll** .... `E`

4. Select/deselect **Lo<u>c</u>k** .... `C`

5. Click **OK** .... `Enter`

Disable/Enable Cell Locking

1. Place cursor in table containing locked cells.

2. Click 🖮 .... `Ctrl`+`F12`
    on Table Toolbar.

3. Select **T<u>a</u>ble** .... `A`

4. Select/deselect **Disable Cell Locks** check box at bottom right of dialog box.

    NOTE: You must use a mouse for step above.

5. Click **OK** .... `Enter`

Table Headers

Sets a specified number of rows in a table (beginning with row one) to repeat at the top of each subsequent page, if a table continues on multiple pages.

1. Select row(s) to contain headers.

2. Click 🖳 .... **Ctrl**+**F12**
    on Table Toolbar.

3. Select **Row**.. **O**

4. Select/deselect **Header Row** check box........... **D**

5. Click [**OK**] .... **Enter**

Set Number Type

1. Place insertion point in table, cell or column in which to set number type.

2. Press **Alt+F12** .... **Alt**+**F12**

3. Select **Cell, Column** or **Table** ....*letter*

4. Choose desired number type option from **Available Types**.

TABLES—SPREADSHEETS

Display Table Formula Feature Bar

Use this when working with spreadsheet functions. Mouse required.

1. Click 🖳 .... **Alt**+**A**, **R**
    on Tables Toolbar.

continued➡

Display Table Formula Feature Bar (continued)

The Formula feature bar appears.

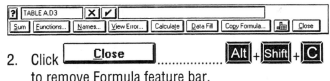

2. Click **Close** .... **Alt** + **Shift** + **C**
   to remove Formula feature bar.

Create or Edit Formula in Table

   —WITH FORMULA FEATURE BAR ACTIVE—

1. Place insertion point in cell to receive formula or
   cell containing formula to edit.

2. Type or edit formula or function .... *formula*
   in Formula text box (to right of check mark button).

*Formula Edit Mode is On appears next to Formula text box.
Formulas can include numbers, operators, cell addresses and
functions.*

Arithmetic Operators	**+**	*(addition)*
	−	*(subtraction or negative)*
	*	*(multiplication)*
	/	*(division)*
	%	*(percent or remainder)*
	!	*(factorial)*
Logical Operators	**=**	*(equals)*
	<	*(less than)*
	>	*(greater than)*
	< >	*or*
	!=	*(not equal to)*
	<=	*(less than or equal to)*
	>=	*(greater than or equal to)*
	&	*(AND)*
	!	*(NOT)*
	|	*(OR) (XOR, similar to IF function)*

continued...

Create or Edit Formula in Table (continued)

Cell Addresses	**A1**	*Cell at the intersection of Column A, Row 1.*
	A1:B7	*A range of cells in column A, rows 1 through 7 and column B, rows 1 through 7.*
Functions	**AVE( )**	*Calculates the average of the values in the cells between the parentheses.*
	SUM( )	*Adds the cells between parentheses to form the total.*
Formula Examples	**E4+E5**	*Adds the values in cells E4 and E5.*
	(E4+E5)/E10	*Adds E4 and E5, then divides the result by the value in E10.*
	SUM(A4:E4)	*Adds the values in A4, B4, C4, D4, and E4.*
	COMM+BONUS	*Adds the values in a cell named COMM to the value of a cell named BONUS.*

NOTE: *You can include cell addresses in formulas by typing them, or by pointing to them with the mouse pointer and clicking.*

3. Click ✔️ to insert formula and turn off Formula Edit mode.

   NOTE: *If WordPerfect cannot calculate formula (i.e., the formula is incorrect), double question marks (??) appear in the cell.*

Set Automatic Calculation Mode

Determines when and what WordPerfect calculates.

1. Place insertion point in table to recalculate.

2. Click 🖼️ .... Alt + A , A
   on Table Toolbar.

   To turn Automatic Calculation mode on:
   Select desired option.

   To turn Automatic Calculation mode off:

   Select **Off**.. O

3. Click 〔 OK 〕 .... Enter

Delete Table Formula

1. Select cell(s) containing formula(s) to delete *(see SELECT TABLE, page 230)*.

2. Select **Table** menu .... Alt + A

3. Select **Delete**.. D

4. Select **Cell Contents**.................................... E

5. Click 〔 OK 〕 .... Enter

Copy Table Formula

1. Place cursor in cell containing formula to copy.

2. Select **Table** menu .... Alt + A

3. Select **Copy Formula**.................................... Y

4. Type address of cell .... *cell address*
   to receive formula.

continued...

Copy Table Formula (continued)

To copy formula down or right specified number of times:

a. Select **Down** .... Alt + D / R
or **Right** text box.

b. Type number of times .... *number*
to copy formula.

5. Click [OK] .... Enter

Ignore Cell During Calculations

1. Place insertion point in cell to ignore.

2. Click 🖳 .... Alt + A , O
on Tables Toolbar.

3. Select **Cell** .... E

4. Select **Ignore Cell When Calculating** .... G
check box.

5. Click [OK] .... Enter

Specify Format of Negative Calculation Results

1. Place insertion point in table to recalculate

2. Click 🔢 .... Alt + A , U
on Tables Toolbar.

3. Select **Custom** .... U

4. Select desired **Negative** .... ↑ ↓
Numbers option.

continued

Specify Format of Negative Calculation (continued)

5. Click [OK] .... Enter

   OR

   Select **Table** .... Alt + A

6. Select **Digits after Decimal** text box ...... Alt + C

7. Type number of decimal digits (1–15) .... *number*
   to calculate.

8. Click [OK] .... Enter

TABS

Set/Clear Tabs

1. Place cursor where tab settings should begin.

2. Click [icon] .... Alt + R, L, T
   on Format Toolbar.

The Tab Set dialog box and the ruler bar appear.

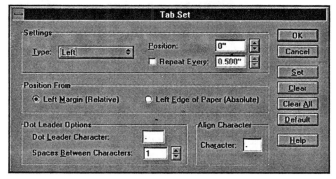

3. Select one of the following **Position From** options:

   • **Left Margin (Relative)** .... Alt + M
     to set tab stops relative to left margin.

continued...

Set/Clear Tabs (continued)

- **Left Edge of Paper (Absolute)** .... `Alt`+`E`
  to set tab stops measured from left
  edge of page.

To clear individual tab stops:

a. Select stop to clear .... `Alt`+`P`, `↑` `↓`
   in **Position** drop–down box.

b. Click `Clear` .... `Alt`+`C`

c. Repeat steps a–b for each stop to clear.

To set evenly spaced tab stops:

a. Click `Clear All` .... `Alt`+`A`

b. Select **Repeat Every** check box .... `Alt`+`V`

c. Enter interval between stops ...... `Tab`, *number*

d. Click `Set` .... `Alt`+`S`

To create individual tab stops:

a. Clear existing tab stops *(see above)*, if
   necessary.

*NOTE: Make sure **Repeat Every** check box is
        deselected.*

b. Select **Position** text box .... `Alt`+`P`

c. Enter tab position .... *tab position*

continued

d. Select **T**ype pop–up list box.... `Alt`+`T`, `F4`

> √ ▲ Left
> ▲ Center
> ◢ Right
> ◢ Decimal
> ▶ Dot Left
> ▲ Dot Center
> ◢ Dot Right
> ▲ Dot Decimal

e. Select desired tab type option `↑` `↓`, `Enter`

f. Click `Set` .... `Alt`+`S`

g. Repeat steps b–f for each tab stop to set.

To change tab type:

a. Select tab stop .... `Alt`+`P`, `↑` `↓`
   in **P**osition text box.

b. Select **T**ype pop–up list box.... `Alt`+`T`, `F4`

c. Select desired tab type option `↑` `↓`, `Enter`

d. Click `Set` .... `Alt`+`S`

To clear all tab stops:

Click `Clear All` .... `Alt`+`A`

To return to default tab settings:

Click `Default` .... `Alt`+`D`

4. Click `OK` .... `Enter`

Change Decimal Align Character

1. Place cursor where new alignment should begin.

2. Click 🗐 .... `Alt`+`R`, `L`, `T`
    on Format Toolbar.

3. Select **Cha_r_acter** text box .... `Alt`+`R`

4. Enter new alignment character .... *character*

5. Click [**OK**] .... `Enter`

TEMPLATES

*A **template** is a reusable document that lets you create an unlimited number of new documents in the customized format. It may contain text, graphics, styles, macros, abbreviations and other elements.*

Select Template

1. Press **Ctrl+T** .... `Ctrl`+`T`

2. Select desired **G_roup** option .... `↑` `↓`

3. Select desired template .... `Alt`+`T`, `↑` `↓`

4. Click [**Select**] .... `Enter`

5. Choose desired options from dialog box, if one appears.

Create Template

1. Press **Ctrl+T** .... `Ctrl`+`T`

2. Select desired **Group** option .... `↑` `↓`

3. Select desired template .... `Alt`+`T`, `↑` `↓`

4. Click `Options ▼` .... `Alt`+`O`, `F4`

5. Select **New Template** .... `N`

6. Insert desired objects, text and graphics *(see below)*.

7. Click `Exit Template` .... `Shift`+`Alt`+`E`
   to close feature bar.

8. Click `Yes` .... `Y`
   to save template.

9. Type template **Name** in text box.

10. Type template **Description** in text box.

11. Click `OK` .... `Tab`, `Enter`

Template Objects

Objects include styles, macros, abbreviations, Toolbars, menus and keyboards. You can create your own objects or use objects already available in WordPerfect.

Edit Template

1. Press **Ctrl+T**.................................... `Ctrl` + `T`

2. Select desired **Group** option .... `↑` `↓`

3. Select desired template........... `Alt` + `T`, `↑` `↓`

4. Click `Options ▼` .... `Alt` + `O`, `F4`

5. Select **Edit Template** .... `E`

6. Edit desired objects, text and graphics *(see above)*.

7. Click `Exit Template` .... `Shift` + `Alt` + `E`
   to close feature bar.

8. Click `Yes` .... `Y`
   to save template.

TEXTART

Creates special text images, including waves, pennants, circles, crescents or bow ties. Images can be further enhanced with shadows, outline text, fills and rotation.

Create TextArt

1. Place insertion point where TextArt should appear in document.

2. Click `ABC` .... `Alt` + `G`, `X`
   on default Toolbar.

3. Type desired text .... *text*
   up to 58 characters on 1–3 lines.

continued

Create TextArt (continued)

4. Select desired TextArt shape on palette.

5. Choose desired option(s) on TextArt feature bar.

6. Click outside TextArt frame to return to document.

Edit TextArt

1. Double–click TextArt .... `Alt`+`E`, `O`
   to edit.

2. Edit image following steps 4–5, above.

3. Click outside TextArt frame to return to document.

THESAURUS

Displays synonyms and antonyms for a specified word and gives you the option of replacing the word or looking up additional ones.

Look Up Synonym or Antonym

1. Place insertion point anywhere on word.

2. Press **Alt+F1**.. `Alt`+`F1`

   To replace word in document with synonym/antonym:
   a. Select desired synonym or antonym.

   b. Click ⎾ **Replace** ⏌ .... `Alt`+`R`

   To show additional related words:
   Double–click any word marked with bullet.

   OR
   a. Select word marked with bullet in list box.

continued...

Look Up Synonym or Antonym (continued)

b. Click **Look Up** .... `Alt`+`L`

WordPerfect displays new words.

To enter word to look up:

a. Select **Word** text box...................... `Alt`+`W`

b. Type word ....*text*

c. Click **Look Up** .... `Alt`+`L`

To review previous Thesaurus search:

a. Select **History** menu...................... `Alt`+`I`

b. Select previous word............. `↑` `↓`, `Enter`
   from drop–down list.

3. Click **Close** .... `Alt`+`C`

TOOLBARS

DEFAULT TOOLBAR

Lets you use the mouse to access frequently used commands and macros.

Select Button on Toolbar

> *NOTE: If the Toolbar is filled, directional arrows appear. Click left or right arrow to scroll to buttons that are not visible.*

Click desired button on Toolbar.

Select Toolbar

1. Select **Edit** menu .... Alt + E

2. Select **Preferences** .... E

3. Double-click Toolbar .... Alt + T, Enter

4. Highlight desired Toolbar .... ↑ ↓, Enter

5. Click **Select** .... Enter

6. Click **Close** .... Alt + C

Display/Hide Toolbar

1. Select **View** menu .... Alt + V

2. Select **Toolbar** .... T

A check mark ✔ next to items on submenus means the feature is active/visible.

Reposition Toolbar

1. Place mouse pointer on blank area of Toolbar or button separator (so pointer changes to a hand icon).

2. Drag bar to desired location.

Copy Toolbar

> NOTE: Toolbars are stored with templates. (See **TEMPLATES**, page 250, for more information.)

1. Select **Edit** menu .... Alt + E

continued...

Copy Toolbar (continued)

2. Select **Preferences** .... **E**

3. Double-click Toolbar .... **Alt**+**T**, **Enter**

4. Click **Copy...** .... **Alt**+**P**

5. Select **Template to copy from** .... **F4**, **↑** **↓**

6. Select Toolbar .... **Alt**+**S**, **↑** **↓**
   to copy.

7. Select **Template** .... **Alt**+**T**, **F4**, **↑** **↓**
   to copy to.

8. Click **Copy** .... **Alt**+**C**

9. Click **Close** twice .... **Alt**+**C**

Create/Edit Toolbar

1. Select **Edit** menu .... **Alt**+**E**

2. Select **Preferences** .... **E**

3. Double-click Toolbar .... **Alt**+**T**, **Enter**

   To create Toolbar:

   a. Click **Create...** .... **Alt**+**R**

   b. Type **New Toolbar Name** .... *name*

   c. Click **Template...** .... **Alt**+**T**

continued

Create/Edit Toolbar (continued)

To indicate where you want to store template:

a. Choose desired option.

b. Click [**OK**] .... Enter

To edit Toolbar:

a. Select desired Toolbar .... ↑ ↓

b. Click [**Edit...**] .... Alt + E

c. Make desired changes:

To create button activating feature:

a. Select **Activate a Feature**.......... Alt + V

b. Select feature .... Alt + E, F4, ↑ ↓
from **Feature
Categories** list.

c. Select feature .... Alt + F, ↑ ↓
from **Features** list.

d. Click [**Add Button**] .... Alt + A

To create icon playing keyboard script:

a. Select **Play** .... Alt + K
a **Keyboard Script**.

b. Type keystrokes ..... Alt + T, *keystrokes*

c. Click [**Add Script**] .... Alt + A

continued..

Create/Edit Toolbar (continued)

To create button launching program:

a. Select **Launch a Program** .... `Alt`+`L`

b. Click `Select File...` .... `Alt`+`S`

c. Select desired file .. `Tab`, `↑` `↓`, `Enter`

To create button playing macro:

a. Select **Play a Macro** .... `Alt`+`M`

b. Click `Add Macro...` .... `Alt`+`A`

c. Select desired file .... *filename*

d. Select macro location .... *location*

e. Click `Select` .... `Alt`+`S`

4. Repeat steps above for each button to create.

5. Choose one of the following options to edit the Toolbar you are creating:

To move button:
Drag it to the new location.

To delete button:
Drag it off the Toolbar.

6. Click `OK` .... `Enter`

7. Click `Close` twice.................. `Alt`+`C`
to return to document.

Change Toolbar Appearance

1. Select **Edit** menu .... `Alt`+`F`

2. Select **Preferences** .... `E`

3. Double-click Toolbar .... `Alt`+`T`, `Enter`

4. Click `Options...` .... `Alt`+`O`

5. Make desired changes.

6. Click `OK` .... `Enter`

7. Click `Close` twice .... `Alt`+`C`

TWO-PAGE VIEW
(See VIEW MODE, page 262.)

TYPEOVER/INSERT MODE

Switches keyboard entry mode from Typeover to Insert. Use Typeover mode to replace existing characters to the right of the insertion point as you type. Switch back to Insert mode (the default mode) for text to move ahead of insertion point as you type.

Press **Insert** .... `Ins`
to switch between Typeover and Insert mode.

> NOTE: *The mode you are in appears at the bottom left of the screen, in the status bar.*

260

UNDELETE

Allows you to view and/or restore your last three deletions.

Restore Deletions

1. Place insertion point where deletion took place.

2. Press **Ctrl+Shift+Z** .... Ctrl + Shift + Z

Last deletion appears as selected text at insertion point.

3. Select desired option(s) on Undelete feature bar.

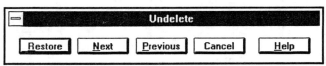

UNDO

Reverses the last change made to a document, such as text you have typed or deleted, or formats you have changed.

> *NOTE: Undo will not reverse some actions, such as insertion point movements, for example.*

Click  .... Ctrl + Z

UNITS OF MEASURE

Allows you to choose between the units of measure WordPerfect uses.

> *NOTE: In this book we have assumed inches as the unit of measure.*

Set Default Unit of Measurement

1. Select **Edit** menu .... Alt + E

continued.

Set Default Unit of Measurement (continued)

2. Select **Pr<u>e</u>ferences**................................... 🄴

3. Click <u>D</u>isplay... Enter

   NOTE: *The **<u>D</u>isplay** icon is preselected.*

   To set default units for dialog box entry and display:

   a. Open **Units o<u>f</u> Measure** .... Alt + F , F4

   b. Choose desired unit .... ↑ ↓ , Enter
      of measure.

   To set default units displayed on status and ruler bars:

   a. Open **Status/Ruler** .... Alt + Y , F4
      Bar Displa<u>y</u>.

   b. Choose desired unit .... ↑ ↓ , Enter
      of measure.

4. Click ⌈ **OK** ⌉ .... Enter

5. Click ⌈ **<u>C</u>lose** ⌉ .... Esc
   to return to document.

   EXAMPLE: *If you enter 72p (72 points),*
   WordPerfect converts it to one inch.

262

VIEW MODES

*There are three different views available to you from the **View**
menu.*

- **D**raft   *Basic text imitates WYSIWYG, but
  features such as headers, footers and
  watermarks do not appear. Therefore, this
  option is usually faster than Page view.
  Press **Ctrl+F5**.*

- **P**age   *Displays a full WYSIWYG. Features such
  as headers, footers and watermarks
  appear. Information that does not print,
  comments for example, appears as icons.
  Press **Alt+F5**.*

  *NOTE: Use **Zoom** (**Alt+V, Z**) to change the display
  size of text or graphics for the above
  options.*

- **Tw**o Page   *Shows two pages at a time. The format is
  similar to Page view, above. Press
  Alt+V, W.*

  *NOTE: Use **Edit**, **Preferences** to set the default
  View mode. (See **PREFERENCES**, page
  170.)*

WATERMARK

Adds a faint image or drawing behind printed text.

*You can have only two watermarks active at one time, though
you may have inserted many more throughout the document.
WordPerfect calls these Watermarks A and B.*

*When you replace a watermark, you must replace it with the
same letter. For example, Watermark A can be replaced by
another Watermark A, but it cannot be replaced by a
Watermark B.*

continued

WATERMARK (continued)

NOTE: *If you create a Watermark A and Watermark B on the same page, they are superimposed.*

Watermark Feature Bar

Appears when you create or edit a watermark.

NOTE: *All watermark procedures are written for the **Page** or **Two Page** view mode. Watermarks can be created from the **Draft** view mode, though you will not be able to view them in it. (See **VIEW MODE**, page 262.)*

Create Watermark

1. Select **Page** or **Two Page** mode from **View** menu.

2. Select **Format** menu .... **Alt** + **R**

3. Select **Watermark** .... **W**

4. Select desired watermark option.

5. Click **Create** .... **Enter**

6. Click **Pages...** .... **Shift** + **Alt** + **A** on Watermark feature bar.

7. Select desired placement option.

8. Click **OK** .... **Enter**

9. Click **Image...** .... **Shift** + **Alt** + **M**

continued...

264

Create Watermark (continued)

10. Type complete pathname........................ *pathname*
    or select from list of graphics.

11. Click **OK** .... `Enter`

12. Click **Position...** .... `Shift`+`Alt`+`P`
    on Watermark feature bar.

13. Select desired **Box Position** option(s).

14. Click **OK** .... `Enter`

15. Click **Close** twice .... `Alt`+`Shift`+`C`

Edit Watermark

Adjusts brightness and contrast, as well as enlarges and rotates watermarks. To make these adjustments, use the image tools palette on the Graphics Box feature bar. (See GRAPHICS, page 76, for more information.)

Move Watermark

1. Place insertion point in first full paragraph of page where watermark should appear.

2. Select **Format** menu .... `Alt`+`R`

3. Select **Watermark** .... `W`

4. Select watermark to move.

5. Click **Edit** .... `E`

6. Click **Pages...** .... `Shift`+`Alt`+`A`
   on Watermark feature bar.

continued

Move Watermark (continued)

7. Select desired placement option.

8. Click [**OK**] .... Enter

9. Click [**Close**] .... Alt + Shift + C

To adjust watermark text shade:
a. Place insertion point inside watermark.

b. Press **F9** F9

c. Enter shade percentage ..... Alt + G, *number*
   (0–100) in **Shading** box.

d. Click [**OK**] .... Enter

Discontinue Watermark

1. Place insertion point in first full paragraph of page
   where watermark should appear.

2. Select **Format** menu.............................. Alt + R

3. Select **Watermark** .... W

4. Select watermark to discontinue.

5. Click [Discontinue] .... D

Delete Watermark

1. Turn on Reveal Codes screen *(see REVEAL CODES,
   page 184)*.

2. Position Reveal Codes window cursor on
   [Watermark A] or [Watermark B].

3. Press **Delete** .... Del

WIDOW/ORPHAN

(See KEEP TEXT TOGETHER, page 115.)

WORD AND LETTER SPACING

Allows you to increase or decrease space between words and letters in a document.

Use the Word Spacing Justification Limits settings to adjust spacing between words in fully justified text. After word spacing limit is met, the spacing between letters will be adjusted. (See KERN TEXT, page 116.)

1. Select text for which you would like to change the spacing.

2. Select **Fo_r_mat** menu .... `Alt`+`R`

3. Select **_T_ypesetting** .... `T`

4. Select **_W_ord/Letter Spacing** .... `W`

5. Choose desired settings:

   - _N_ormal   *Settings from font manufacturer.*
   - _W_ordPerfect Optimal   *Settings from WordPerfect Corporation.*
   - P_e_rcent of Optimal   *Settings you specify.*

   *NOTES: If you choose **P_e_rcent of Optimal**, you must also specify a spacing and pitch. Numbers less than 100% reduce space between words/letters. Numbers greater than 100% increase space between words/letters.*

   If justifying text and words are too far apart, decrease upper limit. If words are too compressed, increase lower limit.

6. Click [**OK**] .... `Enter`

WORDPERFECT CHARACTERS

Provides characters other than those found on the keyboard.

1. Place cursor where character should be inserted.

2. Press **Ctrl+W** ....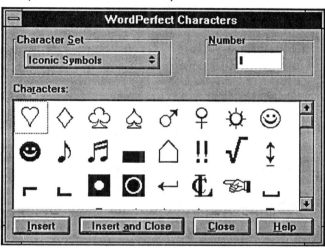
   (WordPerfect Characters).

*—FROM WORDPERFECT CHARACTERS
DIALOG BOX—*

To select from Characters list:

a. Open **Character Set** .... Alt + S , F4
b. Select desired character set .... *letter*
c. Select character .... Alt + R , ↑ ↓
   in **Characters** list box.

To select character by entering its assigned numbers:

a. Select **Number** text box .... Alt + N

continued...

WORDPERFECT CHARACTERS (continued)

    b. Type number (0–14) .... *number*
        of character set.

    c. Press **,** (comma) .... **,**

    d. Type character number in set.............. *number*

    EXAMPLE: 4,8

3. Click **Insert** .... **Alt**+**I**
    to insert character and leave dialog box open.

    OR

    Click **Insert and Close** .... **Alt**+**A**
    to insert character and close dialog box.

WORDPERFECT CHART EDITOR

Open Chart Editor

    —FROM WORDPERFECT DOCUMENT—

1. Select **Graphics** .... **Alt**+**G**

2. Select **Cha<u>r</u>t** .... **R**

   —FROM WORDPERFECT DRAW CHART WINDOW—

    To select chart type:

    a. Select **<u>C</u>hart** .... **Alt**+**C**

    b. Select **T<u>y</u>pe** .... **Y**

    c. Select desired chart type.

3. Make desired changes. *(See following procedures.)*

4. Click **OK** .... **Enter**

Close Chart Editor

Returns you to the document or window you entered from(WordPerfect or Draw).

If you entered through WordPerfect:

Select **C**lose and Return .... `Ctrl`+`F4`

OR

Select **U**pdate .... `Alt`+`F`, `U`

OR

Select E**x**it and Return .... `Alt`+`F4`

If you entered through Draw:

Select **C**lose Chart Editor .... `Ctrl`+`F4`

Select Cell(s)

To select single cell:
Click desired cell.

To select several cells:
a. Position pointer at one end.

b. Drag to other end.

Select All Cells

Click blank cell in upper left .... `Alt`+`E`, `S`
corner of worksheet.

	Legend	A	B	C
Labels		FieldGoal %	Steals	Turnovers
1	Team A	50	14	15
2	Team B	34	10	18

Datasheet

Clear Worksheet

1. Select worksheet.

2. Press **Ctrl+Shift+F4** .... `Ctrl` + `Shift` + `F4`

3. Click [Yes] .... `Y`

Clear Cell(s)

Clears data, format or both from selected cell(s) in worksheet.

1. Select cell(s) to clear.

2. Press **Del** .... `Del`

3. Select desired **Clear** option.

4. Click [OK] .... `Enter`

Edit Cell

1. Double–click cell to edit .... `F11`

2. Enter new **Data** .... *new data*

3. Click [OK] .... `Enter`

Change Chart Type

1. Select **Chart** menu.................................. `Alt`+`C`

2. Select **Gallery**... `G`

3. Make desired changes.

4. Select **Retrieve**....................................... `Alt`+`R`

Change Tiles

1. Select **Chart** menu.................................. `Alt`+`C`

2. Select **Titles** .... `T`

3. Type titles in appropriate boxes..................... *titles*

4. Click `     OK     ` .... `Enter`

Change Number/Date Format

1. Select the worksheet.

2. Press **Ctrl+F12** .... `Ctrl`+`F12`

3. Select desired **Format Type**.

4. Select desired **Formats** option .... `Tab`, `↑` `↓`

5. Click `     OK     ` .... `Enter`

Redraw Chart

Lets you see how changes you make affect your chart.

Press **Ctrl+F3**... `Ctrl`+`F3`

> *NOTE:* *Many dialog boxes also contain a **Preview** button. Before closing the dialog box, select the **Preview** button to see how changes affect the chart.*

Save Chart Style

Saves the style settings (e.g., chart type, etc.) of a chart, separate from the data. Then, when you want to use the same style again, complete **Retrieve Chart Style** *procedure, below.*

1. Select **Chart** menu .... `Alt`+`C`

2. Select **Save Style** .... `V`

3. Type filename .... *filename*

4. Select **Save** .... `Alt`+`S`

Retrieve Chart Style

> *NOTE:* If the Chart Editor is not already open, you must open it. (See **Open Chart Editor**, page 268.)

1. Select **Chart** menu .... `Alt`+`C`

2. Select **Retrieve Style** .... `Alt`+`I`

3. Type filename .... *filename*

4. Select **Retrieve** .... `Alt`+`R`

WORDPERFECT DRAW

Lets you add original graphics to documents. You must use a mouse to access the Drawing Toolbar, which is available through the Draw feature menu. (See also TOOLBARS, page 254.) To learn the function of each draw tool, place the cursor on the desired icon; the tool name pops up to the right of the icon and a description appears in the title bar.

Draw Mode

To display draw tools:

Click  .... Alt + G , D
on Graphics Toolbar.

The Draw window opens with the feature bar at the left and an open screen in the middle.

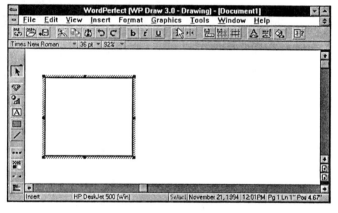

274

Drawing Shapes

The drawing tools (the freehand tool through the square cornered rectangle) require the same basic procedure. Selecting a drawing tool will change the mouse pointer arrow to a crosshair.

—IN DRAW MODE—

1. Select desired tool on feature bar.

2. Position crosshair within drawing area.

3. Click and drag mouse to position where object will end for ellipse and rectangles.

   OR

   a. Click to begin multiple sided figures, arcs and lines.

   b. Move to end of line or side and click.

4. Release mouse button.

5. Double-click to end drawing.

Select Object

*The object is **selected** when it appears to have **handles** in the corners and on the sides. You can then flip, rotate, color, move, copy or delete the object.*

—IN DRAW MODE—

1. Click ▣

2. Position pointer on object and click.

Select Multiple Objects

—IN DRAW MODE—

1. Click ▶️

2. Position pointer on first object to select and click.

3. Press and hold **Ctrl** and repeat steps 1–2 until all objects are selected.

Select All

—IN DRAW MODE—

1. Select **Edit** menu .... Alt + E

2. Click **Se**l**ect** L

3. Select **All** L

Edit Object

You can rotate, copy, flip, fill, color, size and crop objects.

—IN DRAW MODE—

1. Select object(s) to edit *(see page 274 and above)*.

2. Select desired editing preference:

To rotate object:

—WITH IMAGE TOOLS DISPLAYED—

a. Click 🔲 .... Alt + E, O

b. Position pointer on rotate handle 🔄 until pointer becomes a two-headed arrow.

c. Click and drag handle to desired position/angle.

continued...

Edit Object (continued)

d. Press **Esc** .... `Esc`

To copy/paste object:

a. Press **Ctrl+C** .... `Ctrl`+`C`

b. Press **Ctrl+V** .... `Ctrl`+`V`

c. Drag copy to desired location.

To flip object:

Click ▶◀ .... `Alt`+`G`, `F`, `L`

OR

Click ▲▼ .... `Alt`+`G`, `F`, `T`

To fill object:

a. Click 🖼 .... `Alt`+`R`, `I`
   on feature bar.

   OR

   Click 🖌 .... `Alt`+`R`, `I`
   on feature bar.

b. Select desired **Fill Type** from palette.

To size object:

a. Position pointer on handle 🔲 when pointer becomes a two–headed arrow.

b. Click and drag handle until desired size is reached.

continue

Edit Object (continued)

c. Press **Esc** .... `Esc`

NOTE: *To size width and height at the same time, drag a corner handle. To size proportionally, press **Shift** while sizing.*

To change line style/color:

a. Select **Format** .... `Alt`+`R`

b. Select **Line Attributes** .... `N`

c. Select desired **Style** or **Line Color** from palette.

NOTE: *To undo edits, press **Ctrl+Z** or click the **Undo** button on the Toolbar.*

WRITING TOOLS

Grammatik, Speller and Thesaurus are writing tools shipped with WordPerfect. For additional information, please see the individual topics.

ZOOM

Controls the size of on–screen text and graphics. Parameters are 25% to 400%. Otherwise, WordPerfect calculates a percentage based on the following options:

- **Margin Width** *Displays text within window, minimal white space on right and left.*

- **Page Width** *Displays width of page within window, including margins.*

- **Full Page** *Displays all page margins within window (left, right top and bottom).*

continued...

278

ZOOM (continued)

> *NOTE:* *This feature will not change the size of printed text and graphics.*

1. Click `33% ▼` .... `Alt`+`V`, `Z`
   on Toolbar to toggle
   between full page and 100% view.

2. Select desired .... `↑` `↓`
   percentage.

   OR

   Select **Other** .... `↓`, `Enter`, `Tab`, *number*
   and type percentage in text box.

3. Click `    OK    ` .... `Enter`

Set Default Zoom Setting

> *NOTE:* *Use **Display Preferences** to set the default **View/Zoom** setting. (See **PREFERENCES**, page 170.)*

INDEX

283

284

285

290

292

298

Z

FREE CATALOG
_&_
UPDATED LISTING

We don't just have books that find your answers faster; we also have books that teach you how to use your computer without the fairy tales and the gobbledygook.

We also have books to improve your typing, spelling and punctuation.

Tear out the slip below and return it to us for a free catalog and mailing list update.

RETURN TODAY!

- -

More Quick Reference Guides

Access 2 for Win	O-AX2	PageMaker 5 Win & Mac	PM-18
Access 7 for Win 95	AX95	Paradox 4.5 for Win	PW-18
Computer Terms	D-18	PerfectOffice	PO-17
DOS 6.0 6.22	O-DS62	PowerPoint 4.0 for Win	O-PPW4
Excel 5 for Win	F-18	PowerPoint 7 for Win 95	PPW7
Excel 7 for Win 95	XL7	Quattro Pro 6 for Win	QPW6
Internet	I-17	Quicken 4 for Win	G-7
Laptops & Notebooks	LM-18	Quicken 8 for DOS	QKD8
Lotus 1-2-3 Rel. 2.3 DOS	L-18	Windows 3.1 & 3.11	N3-17
Lotus 1-2-3 Rel. 2.4 DOS	K-18	Windows 95	G-6
Lotus 1-2-3 Rel. 3.1 DOS	J-18	Word 6.0 for Win	O-WDW6
Lotus 1-2-3 Rel. 3.4 DOS	L3-17	Word 7 for Win 95	WDW7
Lotus 1-2-3 Rel. 4.0 DOS	G-4	WordPerfect 5.1+ DOS	W-5.1
Lotus 1-2-3 Rel. 4.0 Win	O-301-3	WordPerfect 5.1/5.2	Z-17
Lotus 1-2-3 Rel. 5.0 Win	L-19	WordPerfect 6.0 for DOS	W-18
Lotus Notes 3	O-LN3	WordPerfect 6.0 for Win	O-WPW6
Lotus Smartsuite	SS-17	WordPerfect 6.1 for Win	W-19
Microsoft Office	MO-17	Works 4 for Win 95	WKW4
Microsoft Office for Win 95	MO-95		
Mosiac/World Wide Web	WW-17	**Desktop Publishing**	
MS Works 3 for Win	O-WKW3	Word 6.0 for Win	G-3
OS/2 Warp	Y-19	WordPerfect 5.1 for DOS	R-5

— — — — — — ORDER FORM — — — — — —

DDC Publishing

275 Madison Ave. NY, NY 10016

$10 each
$13 hardcover edition

QTY.	CAT. NO.	DESCRIPTION

☐ Check enclosed. Add $2.50 for postage & handling & $1 postage for each add. guide. NY State res. Add local sales tax.

☐ Visa   ☐ Mastercard   **100% Refund Guarantee**

No._____ Exp. _____

Name_____

Firm_____

Address _____

City, State, Zip_____

Phone (800) 528-3897   Fax (800) 528-3862
SEE OUR COMPLETE CATALOG ON THE INTERNET
@: http://www.ddcpub.com